THE WORLD OF LADY ADDLE

THE WORLD OF LADY ADDLE

comprising
THE MEMOIRS OF MIPSIE
and
LADY ADDLE AT HOME

by
MARY DUNN

With an Introduction by
SIMON HOGGART

ROBIN CLARK LTD
LONDON

Published by Punch/Robin Clark Ltd 1985
A member of the Namara Group
27/29 Goodge Street, London W1P 1FD

Copyright © *Punch* 1945, 1947
Introduction Copyright © Simon Hoggart 1985

Most of the material in *The Memoirs of Mipsie* and
Lady Addle at Home appeared originally in *Punch*, and
is reprinted by kind permission of the Proprietors

British Library Cataloguing in Publication Data
Dunn, Mary
    The world of Lady Addle.
    I. Title
    828'.91407   PR6007.U561/

    ISBN 0-86072-085-3

Printed in Great Britain
by Mackays of Chatham Ltd, Kent

CONTENTS

INTRODUCTION
by Simon Hoggart

Mary Dunn was born in 1900, the youngest of three children. Her father was Arthur Dunn, in his day a considerable sporting celebrity who even played soccer for England. His life story is wonderfully evocative of an age which exists now only in rather improbable fiction, such as that which his daughter wrote. Certainly the attitudes he held and the social world in which he moved must have provided much of the background she used.

Dunn played for Old Etonians in the year they won the FA Cup, 1882, and he laid on the only goal of the match through wizard dribbling down the wing. Mary Dunn later recorded that this had come as a severe shock to the Etonians' opponents, Blackburn Rovers, who had invented what must be the most unlikely terrace chant ever heard in an English ground:

> All hail, ye gallant Rover lads,
> Etonians thought ye were but cads.

Sir Shane Leslie wrote a memoir of him in 1937 in which he said: 'Arthur Dunn taught us to play football as honourably as the game of life, to recite the Kings of Judah and Israel, to love God and to hate Harrow.' Mary added: 'It is possible that life for my father was as simple as that. He was untroubled by religious or philosophical doubts, and would have preferred fixing up coat hooks in the boys' changing-room to any discussion on abstract problems.' He did seem to have been remarkably obsessed by sport, to the exclusion of much else. Sir Shane noted: 'Novel reading in an armchair was his synonym for what was rank and rotten in behaviour.'

He was also an esteemed singer, partly because of the odd fact that his voice did not break while he was at school so that he was able to sing treble until the day he left. Sir Shane records:

> . . . he could have made song his life's work, but was content to give friends a very occasional reminder of his divine gift. In later days I was present at a concert of the conventional type which seldom cheers and never intoxicates. At the last moment someone called on Arthur to sing 'Tom Bowling'. Instead of applause there was dead silence, for the audience was in tears. His voice never broke, but passed from a boy's to a man's.

This event could have appeared almost verbatim in the Lady Addle books – though as it happens Mary also had a good voice and sang briefly with the D'Oyly Carte.

Dunn earned his living as headmaster of a preparatory school he had founded near Cockfosters, called Ludgrove. It still exists, though it has since moved to Wokingham. He married Helen Malcomson, the daughter of a Scottish neighbour, who at first insisted that the wedding could not take place until the school had financial security with ten boys enrolled. He relented at the ninth. Money always seems to have been fairly tight for the family, though there were several upper-class connections of the sort even a penurious Old Etonian might be expected to have. One of the Ludgrove masters became tutor to the Prince of Wales, and one of Mary's godparents was Lady Strathmore, the mother of the present Queen Mother. As a child Mary was taken for tea at Glamis Castle.

Her life seems to have been spent largely in the no-man's-land between the rich and powerful and the genteel middle classes. She married Andrew Shirley, the younger son of the Earl Ferrers, one of whose ancestors was the last peer to be hanged by a silken rope. They too never became wealthy. Andrew could not expect to inherit, and made much of his living as an art historian – in his day he was the acknowledged authority on Constable. It was his second marriage; he had formed an unfortunate misalliance while at Oxford.

The couple went to live at Royal Avenue, Chelsea, in a building which is now a supermarket. It was here that Jane, their only child, was born. They had two servants, a Swiss nannie and a sort of butler who did various jobs. Both of them complained that they could not sleep because of the other's habit of tramping about at night. One evening while they were both out the tramping continued as before, and a clairvoyant was called in to deal with the problem. She announced that the house was haunted by an old man who was guarding it. The spectre was permitted to stay, unlike the manservant, who was sacked, according to family legend, when he was caught wearing one of Andrew's Old Wykehamist ties.

At this stage in their lives Mary had begun her writing career and produced the first of the four *Lady Addle* books. They are by far the funniest work she ever did. Much of her writing was fairly bland, undemanding humour which you might wearily leaf through in a waiting-room. Lady Addle, however, was almost always sharp and cutting.

All the characters, for example, are consumed by their own complacency and self-importance. Secure in their supremacy they know that nothing is too much trouble for other people. Lady Addle thinks of her mother as a saint, for when the girls get scarlet fever, 'she insisted on our nannie remaining with us, night and day for a week, without a second's relaxing of her vigilance'. The family fox terrier becomes old and bad-tempered, so regretfully 'he had to be given to the head groom's children, as he was considered no longer safe to keep'. The premise behind *The Memoirs of Mipsie* is that the British aristocracy can do nothing wrong, pretty well by definition. Mipsie, Lady Addle's sister, is a splendid comic creation. She is variously a thief, a swindler, a fraud, a brothel keeper and a promiscuous adventuress who will do anything to get her hands on jewellery and cash. Lady Addle doesn't excuse her behaviour; it never crosses her mind that there is anything to excuse. Mipsie is an English gentlewoman, and therefore beyond the possibility of reproach.

One of the puzzles about Mary Dunn is that she combined this relish for savage attacks on the upper classes with a considerable and rather snobbish respect for them and their ways. According to Jane, her daughter, she hated hypocrisy and pretension. Yet when Jane said that she wanted to marry Ian Ross, an advertising man, both Mary and Andrew made it clear that they strongly disapproved. It was not, they explained, that they had anything personal against Ian – merely that they hoped for someone with money or a title or, with any luck, both.

When it became clear that the marriage would go ahead anyway, Ian was taken to lunch with Lady Burnham, a family friend on whose estate the Shirleys now lived. 'I was taken to Hall Barn as exhibit "A",' he recalls. 'Afterwards I made the social mistake of sending a thank-you letter. Mary was horrified and told Jane, "you much tell Ian *not* to thank for lunch".' Lady Burnham, however, was very pleased.

Mary and Andrew had moved to the country in 1937, renting Park Hill cottage – actually two cottages knocked together – on the Burnham estate near Beaconsfield. They paid £5 a week, which was a modest rent even then, especially as Mary could often cover much of the amount with an article or a comic poem for *Punch*. *Lady Addle Remembers* had gone through three editions, and its success had made her something of a local celebrity. She liked dressing up, and when Jane held garden fêtes for Dr Barnardo's her mother would open them dressed as 'Lady Park Hill', a role close to her fictional character.

The first *Lady Addle* book was published in 1936, though it was another eight years before she reappeared, this time as a weekly series in *Punch*. *Lady Addle at Home* started its run in the magazine in March 1944, under the title *Lady Addle's Domestic Front*. The war was almost over, and there is an optimistic light-heartedness about the magazine: a political cartoon shows Stalin mounted on a bulldozer, clearing away Nazi rubble. A young housewife asks: 'How would you like your egg this month, dear?'

It is remarkable how many of the people who appeared then are still writing today. Basil Boothroyd, Humphrey Ellis (who wrote the A.J. Wentworth BA books), Richard Price and Paul Jennings were in these issues; David Langdon and J.W. Taylor still draw cartoons. In his history of *Punch*, written in 1957, Richard Price gave one of the very few contemporary written judgements on Mary Dunn:

> She started from the same kind of jumping-off point as several of the rather indistinguishable band of feminine contributors who localized a substantial proportion of *Punch*'s pages in Kensington; but her humour was bludgeoning and destructive, her effects broader. Her most famous series, the mock memoirs of a character called 'Lady Addle' produced rather strained smiles but gave much pleasure to the irreverent. It was cheerful, hit-or-miss fun, and the tone was loud. It made one conscious of how hushed and cloistered the tone in other parts of the paper had become. Lady Addle behaved as no peeress in Angela Thirkell would have behaved, and her creator was allowed an occasional innuendo that it was perhaps assumed would be omitted by Companions reading the articles aloud.

In *Mipsie* at least, the innuendoes are hardly occasional – they occur in almost every chapter and are spelled out with such detail that their excision must have presented Companions with a constant and worrying task.

Lady Addle's Domestic Front must have been thought a success and *The Memoirs of Mipsie* began in February 1945. Mary was paid nine guineas for each article, which seems to have been a decent if not munificent rate. The editor, E.V. Knox, was not one of those who are open-handed with his proprietor's money. People beginning their writing careers, such as A.A. Milne, were told that there would be no fee; it was honour enough to appear in *Punch*. Nor did Knox like to meet his contributors, fearing that personal acquaintance might colour his judgement. Humphrey Ellis, who was his deputy, remembers: 'When it was announced that Mr Someone-or-other had called, Knox might say: 'What *can* the man want?', though the caller had been a contributor for up to ten years.'

Both serializations were published soon afterwards as books, though without the same success as *Lady Addle Remembers* – possibly because aficionados had already read them in the magazine. The last pieces were published as *Round the Year with Lady Addle*, but by this time the humour was less easy. Mary Dunn's skill at taking an ordinary, even banal situation, then suddenly giving it a mad surrealist spin had begun to fade. She did however turn out another good series for *Punch*, called *Shattered Illusions*. On the left-hand side of the page was a set of clichéd incidents in a familiar fictional setting: the artist's garret, the diva's dressing-room, the blacksmith's at Gretna Green. On the right were the same incidents as they might happen in real life. The jokes and parody have the same bite as *Lady Addle*.

The main source for her family of appalling aristocrats must have been that kind of self-serving memoir by a lady of quality which filled many a library shelf then and can still be found today in the older London clubs and second-hand bookshops. Jane thinks that another fund of ideas might have been two of Mary's cousins on her mother's side who lived together in a state of constant social guerrilla warfare. They would bicker endlessly over such questions as which sherry glasses to use.

Though they lived in the same house, they refused to use the same headed notepaper: one spelled the address 'Wealdacre' and the other 'Weald Acre'. They used to dress expensively but in poor taste, and, dowdily attired, would appear at the annual Eton and Winchester cricket match. Jane recalls that her mother was in a state of some anxiety each year until she had tracked the cousins down and paid the necessary courtesies.

They may well have been the inspiration for the terrible social jockeying which appears throughout the books, and Jane believes that they were certainly the source of the bitchy exchange of letters between Lady Addle and her mother-in-law in *Lady Addle Remembers*.

Mary got her pictures from country-house sales, where she would buy boxes and albums full of old family photographs. These were then altered by the publishers, Methuen. Mipsie, whose sister constantly describes her as 'beautiful', is almost always decorated with hideous buck teeth. Again, the ambiguity of Mary's attitude to the nobbish classes emerged: Jane recalls her mother spreading the pictures all over the floor and giggling with pleasure at some particularly grotesque or pompous pose. Then she would say how she hoped that nobody would recognize themselves and so have their feelings hurt.

But Mary's own life rarely brought her close to the likes of Lady Addle. The Shirleys were thought a slightly raffish couple in the London of the thirties and fourties; half Bohemian, half conventional. Mary was invariably dressed smartly if somewhat eccentrically and she favoured lavish wide-brimmed hats. The late Norah Smallwood, who worked with her at Chatto and Windus when Mary was editing a series of brisk career books for girls, said: 'She was quite unflappable. She kept her poise whatever was going on around her. She always seemed to look slightly official, as if she were a lady mayoress about to open a fête.'

One of Jane's friends was Gabrielle Drew, who recalls staying at Park Hill Cottage and being taught how to make mayonnaise, then a rather exotic substance. The Shirleys always served exceedingly generous drinks to their guests, and on this occasion a lot of sherry had been consumed. At one point in the culinary siminar Gabrielle collapsed backwards into a bath. Mary carried on as if nothing had happened.

Hugh Bredin was courting Gabrielle around this time, and used to call in at the flat she shared with Jane Shirley. 'Mary seemed to me at the time a rather buttoned-up person. She would arrive at the flat every six weeks or so, and she usually seemed to have an excuse for not giving the girls advance notice.'

These unannounced arrivals were probably intended to check on the state of the flat, which belonged to Andrew and Mary and was full of excellent furniture – 'highly incompatible', Jane says, 'with a teenage lifestyle'.

Not that Mary was straight-laced. She had told Jane the facts of life and birth control before turning her loose in London – possibly as a reaction to her own mother, Helen, who was both repressive and possessive. She had expected Mary to be home well before midnight every night, even when she was in her twenties. Occasionally Mary dutifully returned, kissed her mother goodnight, then crept out back to whichever party she had left. Years later she told Norah Smallwood that she had given Jane the facts-of-life talk, and this was thought very bold and progressive.

On the other hand, Mary could be equally conventional. Hugh Bredin recalls meeting the Shirleys shortly after they had been to see *Waiting for Godot*, presumably in its first London production. 'They were fulminating that it was all part of some terrible conspiracy to take over Art. Andrew was militantly conservative in these matters, and everything he said was vociferously echoed by Mary.'

Later Bredin met Mary again, and found her light, bubbly and fun – a surprising contrast to the *grand dame* he had encountered earlier. Most people found that she could be sparkling company, when she wanted to be. She wasn't exactly witty, but she did have the knack of giving a humorous cast to any event, however workaday and dull.

The film critic Dilys Powell knew her fairly well: 'She was good-looking though not beautiful, very confident and socially poised. In those days there seemed to be a floating population in London of people who managed to make a living by writing, but who weren't really famous. She was great fun in an impudent kind of way – and she dominated her husband.'

Most of her surviving friends recall this domination, though it's fair to say that's not Jane's memory. At home the relationship was one between equals.

By the fifties she was established as a children's writer. She produced a number of travel books using Jane as the central character, made children's programmes for the BBC, and organized the children's section in book exhibitions. In 1958, Jane made it clear that she intended to marry Ian Ross in spite of her parents' high aspirations. They gave way quickly, with good grace. Jane is still happily married and works as a successful interior decorator. Ian left advertising and now runs the charity International Christian Relief.

Just before the wedding, in 1958, Mary suffered a serious attack of hepatitis and was in hospital during the ceremony. She sent a cheerful telegram signed 'From Your Chrome-Yellow Mummy' and, to Ian's embarrassment, the guests responded by singing 'For She's a Jolly Good Fellow'. A week later she died.

Andrew, miserable with grief and suffering from throat cancer, did not last the year. Jane, who thought of her mother as her best friend, felt angry and horribly cheated.

The Bookseller devoted a full page obituary to her: 'Her keenness was infectious, her energy as prodigious as her versatility, and her direct, practical approach to every problem so inspiriting that difficulties resolved themselves and one found oneself carried away on a tide of mutual enthusiasm.' The writer thought she would be best remembered for her work on children's literature. Lady Addle, after a gap of a dozen years, had been forgotten.

So, outside the family circle, had Mary herself. Dilys Powell says: 'The Shirleys just seemed to vanish from our lives. They would come to dinner, you'd meet them at parties, and suddenly they simply weren't there.'

The rest of the world forgot too, apart from a few people who found copies of *Lady Addle Remembers*, maybe sitting on a dusty shelf during a wet weekend in the country. Then, in 1983, Robin Clark republished the book to a few, but highly enthusiastic reviews. The BBC serialized it on Radio 4 in the autumn of 1984, and the book appeared in the best-seller lists, probably for the first time. Lady Addle, like her own terrible family and the whole of the British aristocracy, had proved indestructible.

THE MEMOIRS OF MIPSIE

MIPSIE ON HER RELEASE FROM PRISON

TO

MY HUSBAND

AN EARLY ADMIRER OF MIPSIE'S

CONTENTS

THE MEMOIRS OF MIPSIE

ILLUSTRATIONS

FOREWORD

By Rear-Admiral The Lord Doomsday, K.C.B., C.M.G.

IT gives me great pleasure to be able to accede to the request of one of my oldest friends, Lady Addle of Eigg, to write a foreword to her memoirs of her remarkable sister. The authoress has a ready pen, and portrays delightfully many incidents and personalities of the good old days, now unfortunately long past, when men were men and women's clothes weren't the wide open spaces they seem to be nowadays. Besides this, Lady Addle can write or discourse on any modern subject with the best, owing to her unusual intellect and insight into human nature. I believe, at heart, she is still the jolly girl she was when I first knew her.

I have known all the Coot girls since they were children, and very jolly girls they were, believe me. Mipsie was always the beauty, of course—she would make every man's eyes, and often his legs too, follow her, even in the street. My grandfather, Admiral Lord Doomsday (every Doomsday has always entered the senior service since the British Navy was created, and most of us have reached flag rank), was Mipsie's godfather, and very fond of her he was, too. He would forgive her anything. 'Fast little ship like Mipsie,' I can hear the old man say with a chuckle, 'bound not to be as steady as one of your "safety first" old tanks with a flat bottom.' At the same time he was old-fashioned enough to be distressed at

1

her many matrimonial disasters. 'Go into dock for re-fitting as many times as you like,' he would say, 'but never change your owner.' He may have been right too. He had only one wife all his life, though I've heard my father say many a time that he wouldn't have recognized her if he'd met her. Once he came back from sea unexpectedly and found my grandmother in the drawing-room. 'What the devil are you doing here?' he roared, for he had a very fine voice. 'How dare you have the infernal cheek to appear on the bridge in my presence?' She explained who she was and he was slightly mollified. 'All right, you can stay,' he said, 'but have the goodness to keep your ugly face turned away from me while I'm in the house.' He was a singularly honest man and always called a spade a spade or a woman whatever he thought she looked at the moment.

When I first met the Coot girls I was a hot-headed youngster of seventeen—a couple of years younger than Mipsie. She took me in hand at once, for I was a bit uncouth and inexperienced in those days, I've no doubt, and I shall always be grateful to her for the things she taught me. We used to go for grand boating picnics on the beautiful lake at Coots Balder. Mipsie had the most appalling memory—she has always been very absent-minded, and many's the time I've known her start off somewhere without an escort and have to stop and pick one up—and she usually seemed to forget that she had left something or other behind at the picnic site, and of course I had to row her back to get it. Then we'd contrive somehow to get late, and often it meant a wigging when we got back from the old man—Lord Coot, who was a bit of a martinet. But I didn't fret. 'Sailors don't care,' was a motto Mipsie implanted in me early.

Soon after that I was posted to Malta and thence to India, so I lost sight of Mipsie for a good many years.

Next time I saw her was in Egypt. She looked splendid on a camel and had the Sphinx beaten to a frazzle. But she did some very rash things which used to worry me a good bit. I remember once seeing her lying in a *dahabeeyah* in broad daylight, dressed only in purple sequins, with a goat bending over her. I've no idea what she was doing. She signalled to me to look the other way, which I did of course, but the whole business worried me a lot. Not long after that she made the mistake of her life in marrying Sir Constant Standing, who was a good fellow, but never had the character to hold a girl like Mipsie. Not perhaps, as I told her at the time, when I asked her to marry me, that I should have been able to keep her either. 'My dear Doom,' she said laughing, 'I don't think even King Midas would be able to keep me.' I asked her who the chap was, never having been a literary bloke myself, and she said, 'He was a man of pure gold,' from which I conclude she meant that a very ordinary sailor fellow like me would never have a chance to win her heart, which I knew only too well.

Not that I gave up the attempt. But it always seemed to be my bad luck to be on high seas when she was between husbands and on *terra firma* when she was tied up. I think the next time I saw her was when she was Princess Ubetskoi. I was a Commodore then, and had to go out on some naval mission to Ekaterinbog. I remember Mipsie immediately sending for me and giving me tea in her 'little boudoir', which was about the size of a battleship's quarter-deck. I recollect feeling a bit nervous, as I know what sticklers some of these foreigners are if one contravenes the customs of their country. But Mipsie didn't care. 'Don't worry,' she said, 'it's an old Mipsian custom and that is much more important.' There was a dark chap there, Prince Michel, her stepson, good-looking, I suppose, in a very un-English and rotten

way. When I went to her boudoir the following day
I found him having tea with her, and I must confess I
was pretty sore. 'Is this a Mipsian custom too?' I
remember asking angrily. 'No,' she said, 'just a custom
of the country.' I felt ashamed of myself then, as
obviously she was only asking the chap out of duty, and
she certainly wasn't the girl to shirk duty, for she asked
him every day, I found out later.

There came a time when I almost won her. I shall
never forget it because in one week I drew the Derby
favourite in the Calcutta sweep, and that same evening
Mipsie, for the first time in her life, told me she would
consider marrying me. I was over the moon with
excitement, as may be imagined, at the possible idea of
achieving a fortune—for the Doomsdays have never
had overmuch of this world's goods—and the girl I loved
at the same time. I suppose that made it seem all the
harder when the favourite wasn't even placed and, two
days later, Mipsie told me she had reconsidered her half-
promise to marry me. I think that was about the only
time I had one over the eighteen, to try and drown my
disappointment.

Now I must give a word to Blanche, who has written
this very talented biography of her sister. She was
always a clever girl, who could put her hand to anything,
and since her marriage she and her husband Addle, who
is one of the best fellows I ever struck, have been really
good friends to me. I used to admire the plucky way in
which Blanche took on, without any training, the cooking
for her household during the difficult times of the last
war. I have often stayed with them at Bengers in the
past few years, and I always made a point of taking down
all my own rations, so as not to add to Blanche's anxieties
by partaking of one dish of her own cooking. So kind
and hospitable is she that she would often try to

press me to taste one, but after my first stay, when I thought it would have been churlish to refuse, I stuck to my guns. Addle and I used to have grand contests at billiards, till Blanche commandeered the billiard table for drying herbs on. He was never what I'd call a first-class player, but a very keen one. His great ambition is to make a break of fifty and I for one hope he will achieve this one day, for he well deserves it for his sportsmanship. Never once when I have finished a break, have I seen him show signs of annoyance at being woken up. 'Let's see, where do we stand now, Doom?' he used to say when he took up his cue once more. A real sportsman and old English gentleman, which is a rarity to-day.

I must end this foreword with a story which is characteristic of Mipsie's warm heart. When the war ended and I retired from the service I thought I would smarten myself up with a lick of paint, so went off to order myself a new suit—quite unnecessarily, as it happens, as I have a whole wardrobe of suits, some as recent as 1920. But my tailor had insisted on reserving a length of pre-war tweed for me, so I thought I may as well have the stuff made up. When completed I put it on and went to take Mipsie out to lunch. Much to my surprise though, she looked quite upset about it. 'What's wrong, old girl?' I asked her. 'Don't you like it?' Mipsie shook her head. 'It's not you,' she said. 'Not the you that I know, that has seen service all over the world and never shirked his duty yet. Please, dear Doom, don't wear it —wear your dear old suits—to please me.' Well, when a girl like Mipsie asks a fellow like me a favour like that, what can one do? But I own I was a bit flummoxed. I don't care much for clothes, but I don't like waste and never have. 'But what am I to do with the blamed things? I've only just ordered them,' I said. 'Send them to me and I'll find a good home for them,' answered Mipsie, which course I accordingly took. About a month later I arrived to fetch her for lunch and something she was wearing struck me as familiar. 'Yes,' she said, laughing, 'it's your suit, converted. Do you really think I would let any one but your best friend wear any garment of yours, Doom?' I was so flattered by that that I believe I should have proposed to her again, at the age of nearly seventy, if she had not just been married to her present husband, Sir Augustus Royster. As it was I contented myself with taking her straight to Cartier's and ordering her a naval crown in diamonds so that, as she suggested, I should nail my colours to the bust, so to speak, of what will always remain the only girl in the world for me.

> DOOMSDAY, Rear-Admiral,
> Conquest Magna,
> Hastings.

I

A METEOR IS BORN

WHAT outward sign does the world give, I sometimes ask myself, to mark the dawn of a great event, a new vital force in its midst? How did Nature acclaim the birth of Julius Caesar, of Napoleon, Nelson—or my sister Mipsie? As regards the last-named, I like to think— for I have ever had a poet's mind—that the famous Balder pink nightingales sang a gayer roundelay that June morning, that the roses in my mother's celebrated moss-rose garden threw off their modest veils for a spell and laughed up at the sun, and that the harebells in the park —it was noted for these lovely flowers, which grew fully three inches high and were of the most beautiful harebell blue—rang a merry peal that day; a pæan of praise for Mipsie.

Indeed, I have often thought that she had something in common with those great men I have mentioned. Like Caesar, whenever she came and saw, she conquered. Like Napoleon, her material gains in Europe were immense. As for Nelson—well, he wore his sleeve pinned on his heart. Mipsie's critics used to say she wore her heart on her sleeve, so frank and impulsive was her nature. So they too have a link, after a century, as I feel sure they would have had if belonging to the same generation. I cannot imagine Mipsie being beaten by a housemaid—especially one without a reference like Emma Hamilton. But I must return to my biography.

Lady Millicent Bertha Geraldine Arabella FitzTartan

Coot, third daughter of the thirteenth Earl Coot, was born at Coots Balder on June 19th, 1871. She was, I think, the only one of us who was not held up for the hounds to sniff, and curiously enough, though love of the chase is part of her very being, and I know her seat has been praised by many competent judges, she alone of our family seems born, I sometimes think, for some softer support than the saddle. She was lovely even as a baby, apparently, with blue eyes like—as my mother said—a misty sea. I, overhearing the words, repeated them in my childish lisp, 'Mip-sea'—and the name became a bedside word in five continents.

Mipsie's godparents included one Royal sponsor— an old custom in our family—Princess Bertha of Nicht-Hinausleen, Lady Geraldine (Diney) Colquholquhoun (pronounced Con), Admiral Lord Doomsday, and dear old Sir Ludovic FitzTartan.

The latter was something of a character. His favourite hobbies were shooting bees, at which he became extremely proficient, though he never, I believe, actually hit one, and racing cockroaches. I shall never forget staying at Sporran Castle, and the thrill of seeing the fascinating little creatures scuttling away from a strong light which was switched on at the starting point of the beautiful course which Sir Ludo had specially constructed for them. All the cockroaches backs were painted different gay colours, like jockeys, and excitement ran high when his guests used to back their favourite runner. But unluckily his best stud cockroach (painted gold) escaped one day into the kitchen, and thereafter the castle became so infested that Lady FitzTartan, who had long sufferingly submitted for years to having the cockroach 'stables' at the foot of their bed, at last put her own foot down, and her husband's life's work had to be abandoned.

Sir Ludo was devoted to his godchild and spoilt her

outrageously. I remember well one time when he happened to be staying at Coots Balder, and Mipsie lost the
beautiful diamond pendant which he had given her at
her christening (she had been dressing up her dolls in
jewels!). She appeared suddenly in the drawing-room,
flung herself on her godfather's knees and confessed the
disaster. He comforted her lovingly, promising to give
her another pendant just like the lost treasure. Mipsie
looked up at him roguishly through her wet eyelids.
'Mipsie bigger girl now—bigger diamonds,' she said.
How Sir Ludo roared! But he took the hint, and the
new pendant was proportionately larger to match Mipsie's
five years. The strange thing was that the original jewel
turned up again not long afterwards, inside a doll's leg.
Those kind of lucky coincidences were always happening
to Mipsie, who certainly had all the good fairies present
at her christening.

And what a christening it was! I was too young to
remember it but it was, I am told, one of the most brilliant
functions of the season. Special trains were run to Little
Balder station, which was festooned in yellow and black
—the Coot colours—so that 'it was just like crawling out
into a gigantic wasp's nest,' as some admirer said. In
addition, there was a Pullman car to bring down dear
Admiral Doomsday, who was crippled with gout, but who
went everywhere in his famous bath chair shaped like a
fo'c'sle. This magnificent but somewhat ungainly vehicle
was engineered into the reception, and the Admiral,
who was a great raconteur and a very popular figure in
any gathering, sat like a Sultan, drinking champagne
diluted with brandy (for he was forbidden wine by his
doctors) out of a silver tankard, keeping every one in
fits by his witty sallies. Suddenly, he surprised the
assembled company by rising, and actually walking,
though rather unsteadily, over to Mipsie, who was holding

a rival court in her nurse's arms. The Admiral drew nearer—then, before any one could stop him, he seized a full bottle of champagne and crying out: 'Come, let's launch this neat little craft,' swung it over his shoulders, and crashed it down on the baby's head!

It was a terrible moment. My mother screamed, and more than one brave man fainted, I am told. But Mipsie holds a charmed life. By an incredible stroke of luck the bottle broke the nurse's arm instead, while Mipsie lay almost untouched, crowing and gurgling with delight as the champagne poured over her tiny face into her mouth. Thus, with a miracle, began the career of one of the famous beauties and outstanding personalities of our time, whose sister I am proud to be, and whose romantic and vivid life history I am privileged to write in these pages.

II

NURSERY DAYS

WE were a high spirited and happy family of children, singularly pure and unspoilt in our tastes, and with an almost austere upbringing in the midst of the splendours of Coots Balder. One wing alone was given to the nurseries. Our daily fare was unvaried—chicken and sole by turns, while no fruit but peaches and grapes was allowed on the table (except during the strawberry and raspberry season, of course) with melons and pineapples on Sundays. We wore simple plush dresses in winter and fine muslin in summer. Our petticoat ribbons followed a rigid pattern as to colour; blue in winter, pink in summer, mauve in Lent. 'I want red—I will have red!' I remember Mipsie saying once, in her lovable commanding way. That night, when the butler poured out my father's port, something stuck in the neck of the decanter. It was Mipsie's ribbons, which she had attempted to dye!

Of course she was no more blamed for that escapade, though it was priceless port, of the most up-to-date vintage that money could buy, no doubt, than she was when she stole one of King Edward VII's spats and buttoned it round her small self, saying: 'I want to know what a royal leg feels like.' Or when she used a whole bottle of a visiting duchess's French scent to put behind the ears of her pet dog, Rascal, a delightful fox terrier puppy, beloved by us all. Alas, when he grew up his temper became uncertain and he had to be given to the head

groom's children, as he was considered no longer safe to
keep.

What a happy place was nursery land and what exciting
games we used to think out, for we were unusually
intelligent and original children, I believe. Hide and
seek, hunt the thimble, cobbler cobbler, kiss in the ring.
Even Papa, who underneath his rather forbidding manner
had all the enthusiasm of a boy, used to delight in playing
this when he sometimes brought visitors up to the nursery,
or even when alone. We had a very pretty nursery maid
called Eva, with lovely golden curls and a face like a
cherub. In fact we used to call her 'the Angel' because
she looked exactly like a picture of angels saving a sheep
from falling down a well, which hung in the nursery.
Papa always insisted on her joining in too, for he was often
quite democratic in his views I have noticed, so we were
a splendid party. The mention of angels reminds me of
a story of Mipsie which I specially love. One night she
slipped out of bed and stole along to the day nursery to
retrieve a favourite doll which Nannie had hidden as a
penalty for some childish misdeed. But Mipsie knew
just where it was—she was so clever in those ways—and
also that Nannie would be downstairs having supper.
However, she returned, to my surprise, without it—
and looking rather thoughtful. Silently she climbed into
bed. Then, after a pause: 'Blanche,' she said. 'Can
angels sit on people's knees?' I considered the point,
having always been interested in theology from a child.
'I don't really know, darling,' I remember saying, 'but
I shouldn't *think* so.' 'That's just where you're wrong,'
said Mipsie. 'They can' but not another word could I
get out of her on the subject. What wondrous celestial
vision had been vouchsafed to a child's innocent believing
eyes that night, I wonder?

Most of our youth was spent in our historic and beau-

MIPSIE AT 'THE AGE OF INNOCENCE'

tiful home, but every summer we went to stay with some
Scottish cousins, the McTott of Rum and Lady Agnes
McTott on their beautiful island adjoining Eigg, my
husband's native soil. It is strange to think I must have
met him, for he often used to come over for picnics.
Indeed, I remember a sturdy freckled boy finishing off
a beautiful sand castle near us one day, and then my
brother Humpo, who was adorably mischievous, taking
a flying leap on to it! The older boy immediately put
down his iron spade and picked up a bucket, so as to
hit Humpo's head with something less heavy. I recollect,
even at that early age, being struck by such gallantry.

Another memory of Rum comes back over the years,
and one that still makes me shudder.

On that rocky and sometimes treacherous coast, the
tide often turns unexpectedly and creeps in with the pace
of a galloping snail. One day, I was lying on the shore
absorbed in a book, when happening to glance up, I
saw Mipsie, some twenty feet distant, perched on a big
rock. Suddenly I remembered with horror that the tide
was almost on the turn. In half an hour it might reach
Mipsie's rock. In an hour it would undoubtedly have
surrounded it.

What should I do? Should I go and tell Nannie,
sitting beside the sleeping Humpo under the shade of the
cliff near by? Or should I dash round the bay to the
village and rouse one of the fishermen from his afternoon
nap? But both courses would take time, and time was
the vital factor. Within five minutes I had made up my
mind. I would go to Mipsie's aid myself.

Swiftly I made my way over the sharp rocks and urged
my little sister back, saying only that tea was ready, so
as not to alarm her. When we reached Nannie I sank
down, I remember, trembling a little with shock. But
youth is resilient, and a good tea soon put me right.

As we ate it though, I watched the cruel waves coming nearer and ever nearer to the rock on which Mipsie had stood so lately. When we left the beach some forty minutes later I glanced back. The rock was entirely covered. I breathed a little prayer of thankfulness as I looked at my beloved sister, dancing gaily ahead, blissfully unconscious of her amazing escape from a terrible death.

III

DIFFICULT YEARS

'WHEN a man marries his troubles begin,' runs the old saying, but a woman's troubles begin far sooner, especially if she is beautiful, and poor Mipsie was soon to learn something of the unkindness and misunderstanding from a harsh world which is ever the lot of fair women.

The first unlucky incident was in 1886, when she was fifteen. A new curate—a Mr. Basil Simpson—had just come to Balder. Young, extremely handsome and a fine preacher, he was also exceptionally modest, and seldom looked up from the book of sermons which he read so delightfully. When he did, it was to encounter, in the front pew, the rapt and fervent gaze of one, at any rate, of his hearers. Mipsie, at an impressionable age, was just beginning to experience the emotions and aspirations of budding womanhood. What more natural than that she should be deeply stirred by this new influence? My mother welcomed the signs of a serious outlook in one who, though sweet, had been inclined to be frivolous hitherto, especially when the change was accompanied by a touching humility. Although our religious instruction was all that could be desired—having been undertaken by Mama herself—Mipsie declared that she would 'like to begin all over again,' and begged to be allowed to attend Mr. Simpson's Sunday classes. Accordingly, she and I went every week, for an hour—and then very often Mipsie would think of some point on which she needed further enlightenment, and would make me wait at the

door of the Church Hall while she ran back to her instruc-
tor. She had, of course, even at that age, a fine sensitive
mind which took a deeper view than did my humbler
brain.

So passed spring and summer and eventually we came
to Harvest Festival, in which of course we, as the great
house, invariably played a predominant part.

My eldest sister Soppy[1] was always in charge of church
decorations. None knew better than she just how to
choose the softest evergreens for the lectern at Christmas,
so that my father could read the lessons without being
pricked (she kept the holly for the choir), or that the vicar
had a dread of anything that harboured earwigs. No one
could make a sheaf of corn 'stay put' as she could. She
was older than us so had had practise with the then
fashionable hair 'chignons' of course.

But on this occasion Mipsie insisted on going too, so
off the two girls went and returned, after three hours,
tired but satisfied. What was our consternation, however,
on entering our pew next morning, when the first thing
that greeted our horrified gaze was a huge vegetable
marrow, reclining against the curate's stall, painted in
clear letters: 'I LOVE YOU' followed by two hearts
intertwined and the initials M.C. and B.S.? Who was
the perpetrator of the odious joke we never knew—
doubtless some jealous village girl—but it was considered
by Papa to be too invidious to pass unnoticed. Mr.
Simpson was consequently removed, and lest Mipsie
should be further subjected to tricks in such bad taste,
she and I were sent, after over a hundred prospectuses
had been perused, I believe, to Miss Clamp's well-
known school in Shropshire.

It was strange, after always having had our own
governesses to order about as we pleased to be one of an

[1] Sophia, Lady Hogshead.

MYSELF AND MIPSIE IN OUR TEENS

obedient crowd; to wash in a plain white toilet set without the familiar coronet, to walk on grass instead of lawns. Strange—but not unpleasant. The girls were dears and I made lasting friends with several, even one who was a brewer's daughter, though I fear I kept this from Mama! But she afterwards married a baronet so all ended well. As for Mipsie, she soon became a little queen in the school, and whatever she did became the fashion. But once again, alas, her very charm and outstanding personality led to trouble.

The pupils' reading was very strictly guarded by Miss Clamp. Nothing in the nature of a novel was allowed to enter the school, let alone magazines, which were considered dangerous in the extreme. This struck Mipsie as narrow minded—she was ever the champion of liberties of all kinds—and she soon started to collect books by Ouida, Miss Braddon and others, also to write regularly to *The Girl's Own Mag.* under *nommes de plume* such as 'Bashful Husband', 'Enquiring Kitten' or 'Keyhole Kate', the letters being posted through the agency of a servant. The replies and the novels Mipsie kept in an old chest in a boxroom. There was a big demand naturally— in fact Mipsie was forced to charging sixpence for loans, which worried me a little till she told me she was saving the money for foreign missions. She was thus the founder of all lending libraries, only for a worthy cause— a typical stroke of genius.

All would have continued well, had not the oak chest been needed for some theatricals. The unusual weight aroused suspicion, the lock was forced open (for Mipsie kept the key) and the contents were discovered!

It was her sweet unselfishness that saved my sister. For she had had, a few days previously, that kind of presentiment that sometimes comes to brilliant people, that she might not be long in the school. Accordingly she

had inscribed the name of every girl in the school—
except ours—on the fly leaves of every book, so that each
schoolfellow should have some memento of her. It was
a generous and loving act which repaid the donor a
thousandfold; for of course the books were not associated
with her, and yet it was impossible to punish the whole
school. Had Mipsie been a man she would surely have
been an ambassador by now?

The whole episode would have passed with a stern
reprimand, had it not been that right at the bottom of
the chest were suddenly found—*two French novels*. Miss
Clamp, I heard, fainted right off at the discovery. When
she recovered she summoned the whole school. 'Girls,'
she said sternly, 'this matter is no longer one of indiscre-
tion and unladylike behaviour. It is one of crime. It
must be sifted to the very bottom.'

IV

FINISHING TOUCHES

THE night after the discovery of the hidden books, including the two French novels, I slept badly, tossing and turning in my worry about what an investigation might bring to my poor innocent sister. Suddenly I woke to find her beside me, the candle lighting up her lovely hair, which was very luxuriant, hanging well below her neck and always shining with a perfectly natural grease.

'Get up and pack your trunks, Blanche,' she whispered. 'We are leaving to-morrow.'

'Leaving!' I gasped. 'But why?'

'I will not have any one wrongfully accused of hiding French novels,' said Mipsie staunchly. 'We must leave as a protest.'

So next morning we marched, she boldly, I in some trepidation, into the headmistress's sanctum.

'My sister and I are leaving,' announced Mipsie. 'We do not care to be associated with a scandal in any school.' Miss Clamp went as white as her shirtfront.

'But, Millicent,' she protested. 'No reflection was cast upon you or your sister. Yours were the only names not found in the books.'

'No matter,' said Mipsie. 'It is a deeply shocking occurrence, and I shall tell my Mama and Papa that we were unable to remain in such surroundings.' Miss Clamp turned as grey as her hair.

'Pray, pray, Lady Millicent, do not do that,' she begged.

19

'It will reflect badly on the school if Lord and Lady Coot hear such a thing.'

Mipsie, who had turned to the door, paused on the threshold. 'Will you promise us that there shall be no investigation, and that this odious business shall never be mentioned again, then?' she demanded sternly. There was a moment's pause. Then:

'I promise,' said Miss Clamp, flushing as red as the exercise book in her hand.

When we eventually left school, we were warmly embraced by the teachers and given quite a little ovation by the girls, some of them giving us lovely parting presents which they had made themselves—a beautifully-enamelled drainpipe parasol-stand for Mipsie, and a photo frame with real lace curtains for me. What a thrill to unpack these, and our prizes, and gloat over them. Suddenly, in Mipsie's pile of books, I saw, to my astonishment, the two confiscated French novels!

'Mipsie!' I gasped. 'However—wherever?' Mipsie smiled her most elfin smile.

'I knew just where to look for them,' she said. 'They were by Miss Clamp's bedside.'

There now followed a rather 'odd job' period of governesses for Mipsie alone, as I was eighteen and just about to come out. The trouble with these well-meaning but touchy people was my brother Humpo, who was, of course, a decided tease. During term he was at Eton (though he was nearly expelled for damping all the fire-works for the Fourth of June), but in the holidays the troubles began—specially with the French governesses. How Mdlle. Pinard screamed when she found her powder-puff full of wood lice!—it served her right for her Frenchi-fied ways, Humpo said, with that subtle satiric wit that distinguished him even at that age. And how we screamed —but with laughter—when Mdlle. Boudin opened a box

which she thought contained a new jacket, and found—
a dead cat! She was ill for days!

Eventually, after ten or twelve governesses, Mipsie
implored to be allowed to complete her French education
in Paris. Mama opposed this, I remember, fearing the
dangers of foreign food and Roman Catholicism; but
Papa, rather surprisingly, advocated it strongly, even
volunteering to take and fetch Mipsie each time, staying
a week or two in Paris till she felt 'settled in'. Accordingly, in the summer of 1888, Mipsie went to St. Germain
'to be finished'.

The use of this expression reminds me of an amusing
story of an old gardener of ours called Bobbin, a path
weeder I think (all our weeds were lovingly extracted by
hand by our devoted garden staff—no weedkiller for
them!). Bobbin asked me after Mipsie one day. 'Why,'
I told him, 'she has gone to Paris to be finished, Bobbin,'
'Dear, dear, is that so?' asked the old man sympathetically. 'Her ladyship being what she is that wouldn't
take long in Paris, I reckon.'

I don't remember many details of Mipsie's school life
in France, as I was by then in the whirl of my first season.
But her letters home were radiantly happy, and of course
she did brilliantly in class, as usual, soon being head of
the school except for nine others. She also started to
take a sudden interest in music, and put in long hours
in the solitary music room. 'I am advancing so fast,
Blanchie,' she wrote, 'that I have now graduated from
Fräulein Lauch to Monsieur Poirot, the wonderful young
professor here.' Next winter she wrote even more enthu-
siastically, 'I am learning all the *études* with the professor,
and love my lessons. Only Paris is dreadfully cold. But
he is so inspiring, and such a great musician. Sometimes
he sings "Your tiny hand is frozen" to me and acts it all
too beautifully for words.'

She left somewhat suddenly in consequence of a stupid misunderstanding. Mipsie always adored history, and she was thrilled with the excursions to Versailles, St. Cloud and other places of historical interest. So immersed was she in the past that she took the trouble to find out just what part of the Bois de Boulogne Madame de Pompadour frequented every day, in the same blue dress, in order to attract Louis XV's attention, and spent one whole afternoon near the same spot in order to steep herself in the historical atmosphere. Unluckily she was seen by the head of the *pension* who, completely mis-contruing Mipsie's action, demanded her instant removal. It is so like the narrow scholastic mind to fail in appreciation of the born student of history.

V

COMING OUT

WHAT an auspicious event this was in the good old days, and how different from the present time, when a girl's figure scarcely changes with her début, and young people seem old before their 'teens. 'Do you mind awfully if I cut Lords this afternoon, Grandpapa?' my grandson said to Addle just before the war at the Eton and Harrow. 'There's a new film I want to see.' I was somewhat shocked, I must confess, but Addle said nothing. Indeed, he is inclined to be taciturn during a cricket match, and often his only remark during a whole day is 'Wait till the end of the over, dear.' (I suppose he thinks, in his old-world, courteous way, that the players would have to stop their game if I get up from my seat. He is always so considerate.) I am very fond of watching cricket myself, when with a cushion and a congenial companion one can spend the pleasantest afternoon, chatting of times past and present.

To return to girls' figures in the 'eighties, what miracles of elegance and womanliness they were. The tiny waist, the soft curves above and below, the smart bustle behind. I must admit, though, that the right effect was not achieved without trouble and sometimes tears. Gone were the days my mother knew, when she used to lie on the floor while an exceptionally strong footman (blindfolded of course) used to place one foot in the small of her back and lace her up. But a figure was still sufficiently important, in 1889, for Elsie Rye (Lord

Peckham's elder daughter), on the eve of her coming out ball, to get her young sister to hammer in a croquet hoop round her waist while she lay on the lawn.   Unfortunately the sister was then called in to bed and poor Elsie lay the whole night pinned to the damp grass and had pneumonia next morning. Another friend, Lady Mary Linsey-Wolsey, who had the misfortune to be very flat-chested, bethought her of wearing an air cushion inside her dress; but in the crush of a reception she unwisely mounted a chair—some one's hatpin punctured the air cushion, and the whole crowd looked on in horror while her corsage collapsed with a long whine.

Another trial was hair.   Fashion demanded a hair style which needed great luxuriance of woman's glory, and although of course we Coots all had beautiful hair, others were not so blessed, and were forced to wear false switches or coils pinned on.   (I hope my male readers will not be shocked to hear of this deception.) My cousin Clara Twynge was very unlucky in the management of hers.   They kept slipping off, once into the offertory plate, and once into a jug of fruit cup at a ball, which added somewhat to her natural shyness. Indeed, between that and the fact that she was distinctly plain (I do not know why, for she was a close cousin of ours), she was scarcely ever asked for a dance, and some unkind girls dubbed her 'Cloakroom Clara' because she used to spend almost every evening in that sad spot. Eventually Mipsie heard of this, and with her usual warm-hearted sympathy soon put things to rights.   At the next ball, when Clara entered the ballroom, all eyes were drawn to a card attached to her bustle: 'Still waters run deep.'   That evening she was besieged with partners and received three offers of marriage, all of which, in her shyness, she accepted, which was fortunate as two of the suitors threw her over next morning.

LE DUC DE TIRE-BOUCHON

Even in that age of beautiful women Mipsie's entrance into Society created something of a sensation. '*Qui est cette demoiselle là?*' asked the French Ambassador, a great connoisseur of beauty. When informed he said simply '*Tiens*' and continued to look at Mipsie. Even his Gallic eloquence was silenced by such loveliness, it seems. The same evening H.R.H. the Prince of Wales —afterwards King Edward VII—was evidently much struck with her. She happened, in the supper-room, to drop her fan almost at his feet. In a flash he had picked it up and handed it to her. A few minutes later she tripped on the staircase (she trips very easily I have often noticed) and his was the hand that came to her rescue. 'You are unfortunate this evening, Lady Millicent,' the Prince said gravely, while Mipsie blushed vividly at the compliment implied. A royal memory for faces is well known of course, but Beauty in Distress had evidently made an indelible impression on her future sovereign.

But, indeed, Mipsie was always the pet of Royalty. Her flashing wit and brilliant repartee often saved some difficult situation and turned a frown from a Royal brow. I remember one party at the Royal Yacht Squadron garden during Cowes week, when the somewhat austere King Crustatian of Iceland was the guest of honour. A sudden thunder shower had turned all the milk sour and H. M. was disposed to be annoyed, when: 'There shouldn't be any shortage of milk at *Cowes*,' said Mipsie audaciously. The Royal displeasure suddenly melted into a smile while every one blessed Mipsie for the quick wit that relieved the tension.

On another occasion she was able to do great service to her country by saving an Eastern potentate from an embarrassing episode. During a house party at the Duc de Tire-Bouchon's lovely château for the Chantilly Races, the vastly rich Great Curd of Bokhara had ordered a beautiful butterfly brooch to be carried out in rubies, amethysts and emeralds, the Duc's racing colours, as a gift for the Duchesse.   This lovely jewel was to be placed, as a charming whimsy, in a naturalistic manner amongst the flowers at dinner.   But the jeweller had made a mistake and used sapphires instead of amethysts.   There was a nervous pause while every one looked at the butterfly and wondered what was wrong, for the Curd's face was like thunder.   Then Mipsie, suddenly realizing the situation, took the brooch and swept him a deep curtsey.

'I am honoured, your Highness,' she said, 'both by the gift and by your gracious memory of our armorial colours.'   It was a brave, splendid lie (for the Briskett colours are red and silver), told so as to save a foreign power from embarrassment.   Relations were distinctly strained between our two countries at the time, so who knows what political strife, or worse, may have been averted by her noble action?   But that is not the only time my dear sister, by her tact and brilliance, has helped her country, I am proud to say.   At one time she was known as 'The Foreign Office Bag,' so many statesmen and State secrets did she hold in the palm of her lovely hand.

VI

ENGAGEMENT

ALTHOUGH my dear father and mother naturally wished to see their daughters married well, they were sufficiently idealistic in their attitude to matrimony to leave us entirely free in our choice, only stipulating that we should marry into the peerage (indeed we scarcely knew any one outside it so this was a needless precaution) and that our future husbands should have not less than £10,000 a year, so that we should be spared the misery of finding out for ourselves that 'Love flies out of the window when Economy comes in at the door' as the old saying goes. 'Ah, my dear,' I recollect an elderly lady saying to me when I was about twenty years of age. 'No one who hasn't experienced it knows the agony of soul that poverty and squalor bring.' She was speaking of the sale of their beautiful steam yacht which had to be effected before her husband could purchase one slightly larger.

My father was perhaps slightly more ambitious for his children than Mama was. I remember his referring to a certain German Prince who sought Mipsie's hand as 'jumped-up eighteenth century Royalty' and on another occasion he nipped in the bud what might have been a serious romance between myself and the very eligible Lord Gordon Dramm, heir to the marquisate of Deoch and Dorris. 'Gor,' in spite of his strict Scottish up-bringing, had grown up decidedly unconventional, and was rumoured to be friendly with writers and even, some said, *artists*, though it doesn't do to believe all one hears.

27

Apart from this there was nothing serious against him, and he was the jolliest person imaginable, entering into every social function with great gusto and spirit. He had begun to single me out for special attention (giving me once, with lithe impetuosity, a sprig of white heather), and it must be admitted that I was equally taken with him. But one evening, at a dance at my old home, Coots Balder, I was waltzing with another partner and looking out (as girls will!) for my special admirer, when I saw a sight that froze the bones in my marrow. Gor was waltzing with another girl—and *he was reversing*! Immediately the dance finished I fled to my room and flung myself on my bed in floods of tears. Next morning Gor left, after a stinging rebuke from Papa, who afterwards told me never to mention the name of 'that bounder' again. It all shows what can happen to the best people by getting into the wrong company. Now, of course, I bless Gor for that solecism. I am sure my dear Addle has never done anything dishonourable or ungentlemanlike in his life. (Apart from anything else, he has never been sufficiently quick on his feet to manage the waltz at all.)

Perhaps it would be of interest to quote here two letters of my father's and mother's concerning Mipsie's future, which show the infinite and loving care with which parents in those days watched over their children's lives.

House of Lords, October 3rd, 1890.

MY DEAREST ARABELLA,
  'I have made inquiries about young Harborough. He has 15 thou. it is true, but his estate is heavily encumbered, and his pedigree cattle and his mother cost him too much. They say Ld Skein is a warm man. He is too old for an heir probably, so Mipsie could marry

again when he dies, or better still live with us and could enlarge the west wing as I have always planned. On the whole, however, I favour Briskett, even if his money is made in meat. He has the best moor in Scotland and a fine house in town next door to my club.

'Yr affectionate husband,

'C.'

Coots Balder, Oct. 6th.

'MY DEAR BOGGLE (my mother's pet name for Papa),

'I recd your letter yesterday and hasten to reply. Dearest, do you really think that the Duke of Briskett would make Mipsie happy? Money is not everything, and I cannot bear to think of our dear girl in those stone corridors at Briskett Castle. I know I should never feel anything but shivery there myself. Have you thought about young Ld Bodmin? Such a lovely place, as good as the Sth of France (you know what a shocking sailor I am) and I hear he is a nice young man, though illiterate they say, but of course Mipsie would manage all his affairs for him. I beg you not to decide in a hurry. Mipsie's happiness is all that matters to both of us, I know.

'Yr devoted,

'NIBBLES.'

(My father's pet name for Mama.)

'PS.—I am told the Bodmin fishing is superb.'

Eventually, as all the world knows, Papa's wishes for Mipsie's future prevailed over those of my mother, and my sister became engaged to 'Oxo' Briskett. She herself seemed oddly indifferent on the subject. I recollect her saying, with a strange bitterness for one so young, that she was beginning to find out that all men were made on much the same pattern. Yet I think she was happy in those engagement days. We used to have great fun opening the shoals of beautiful presents in the Orangery. Mine was the task of jotting down the shop labels on each present, so that they could be returned later if desired, for Mipsie was far too considerate to return them to the donors direct. Apropos, I cannot resist concluding with an amusing story of Mipsie's only slip in thanking for a gift.

It chanced that two Royal Dukes had both sent her a cake basket, Duke A's being of gold and Duke B's of silver. Mipsie *muddled up the Dukes* (an easy mistake to make) and wrote the following to Duke B.

'I shall think of your Royal Highness every time I use your beautiful gift, which will be daily, as I love gold filigree above everything, and although I have been given a silver basket shall never look at it, for it is far inferior in workmanship and material to your Royal Highness's.'

A second exquisite gold filigree cake basket arrived by special courier next morning!

VII

MARRIAGE

OF Mipsie's wedding day I can say little, for I myself was in such a whirl that I actually walked up the aisle after her in goloshes with my dainty peacock merino brides-maid's dress! The service was solemn and beautiful in the extreme, every stone of the lovely old Balder Church, set off to perfection by the cream of Debrett, every flower that Heaven—and our famous hothouses—had created, reflecting the splendour of the occasion. Yet it was all quite simple. Two bishops and one archbishop only performed the ceremony. A humble bandsman from Oxo's regiment played 'Ave Maria' on the bass trombone; while the bridegroom, for all his wealth and many titles, stood alone, save for his best man, at the chancel steps, just like any ordinary wedding. Thus, in that simple country setting, my sister Mipsie gave her hand to a man who never really attempted to understand her, or to appreciate her amazing qualities.

Things really started going wrong, Mipsie tells me, as early as their honeymoon, which was spent at Kings Maunders, the beautiful and romantic home of Lord Dotage, which had been lent for that supposedly happy time. One afternoon, Oxo could not find Mipsie any-where and after a long search discovered her in a spinney talking to a young man who rented some of the shooting, under the impression that it was her husband. The two men were of much the same height, both fair with small moustaches, and Mipsie had only been married two days.

It wasn't such a very serious mistake to make—but Oxo immediately took umbrage, as he always did at the adorable vagueness which was part of her charm.

The next quarrel was about the house. It must be explained that although the dukedom of Briskett was comparatively recent, the family of Loigne[1], as Earls of Chine[2], had lived in historic Briskett Castle in Northumberland since the Conquest. Queen Elizabeth had stayed awake all one night in the State bedroom[3], King Charles II[4] had shot an oak-apple off his brother's head in the park, Perkin Warbeck[5], as a scullion in the Briskett kitchens, had served up the meal which caused Henry VII[6] never to smile again. Several well-known ghosts also lived there.

But fine though the castle undoubtedly was, it was an austere and depressing place for a young bride of nineteen, and Mipsie can hardly be blamed for attempting to cheer it up somewhat. Her faultless taste naturally led, after her recent stay in Paris, to French décor, and so she had graceful Louis Quinze legs fitted on to the clumsy oak refectory tables, the fan vaulting of the Great Hall painted in the style of Boucher, and turned one of the dungeons into a *Salle des Glaces* as a compliment to Versailles, besides making a torture chamber into a very cosy little visitors' bathroom. She also gave orders for sprays of orchids to hang from the vizors of the suits of mail— for she just couldn't live without orchids, so great was

[1] Sometimes spelt Loyne or even Lohoyoillen.

[2] The Eighteenth Earl was awarded a dukedom for his brilliant work in remembering the names of all Queen Anne's children.

[3] The last person who actually slept there was Oxo's grandmother, who afterwards died of a fractured pelmet.

[4] Also dead.

[5] See Lambert Simnel.

[6] Who completed the famous chapel at Westminster, begun by Henry VIII during the Reformation.

her love of Nature—and bunches of carnations and roses to be placed daily in the jaws of the various skin rugs which lay all over the castle, for Oxo's father had been a keen big-game hunter. When Oxo seized an armful of these lovely blossoms and threw them into the fire, Mipsie immediately realized, with her delicate feminine intuition, that he was displeased, and essayed to mend matters by taking the best rug in the collection, a magnificent snow leopard, and having it made into a cloak in compliment to the father-in-law she had never seen. Could graceful tact go further? But this only seemed to make Oxo more angry still. He forbade her to alter the castle any more, saying that what was good enough for his ancestors was good enough for him. 'Of course, dear. Too good.' Mipsie said soothingly, but for some unaccountable reason that charming tribute to his forefathers was the last straw. Oxo flung himself out of the room, as he went breaking off the ormulu top which Mipsie had had fixed to a Saxon halberd and hurling it out of the window. It was their first real quarrel.

I have mentioned the Briskett ghosts. These included the headless third earl, who was said to walk the long gallery every night. For generations a beaker of brandy and a biscuit had been laid out for him each night by the butler. Brandy and biscuit were always gone by morning. But Oxo's mother, who was Scottish, thought the custom extravagant and silly and stopped it. The butler immediately gave notice. It is rather touching to think how much family tradition meant to servants in those good old days.

Then there was at one time a white stable cat which was said to have jet-black kittens every time one of the Loigne family died. But there was, I believe, some other explanation of that phenomenon not connected with the supernatural. Lastly, there was the famous Red Sultan, whom Mipsie actually saw.

The sobriquet was given to the seventh Earl for his oriental habits and character, which were known for miles around. He was eventually murdered by an irate farmer who discovered his daughter—a maidservant in the castle —dancing on the dining table before Lord Chine, dressed entirely in strings of coral. The ghost, apparelled in gorgeous Eastern robes and smoking a hookah, is said to haunt a room in the North Tower, which is consequently never used. But one day, both Mipsie and 'Weed' Wastrel (Sir Arthur Wastrel, an old admirer of hers, so nicknamed for his habitual cigar), announced their intention of keeping watch for one night in the haunted room. They tossed—and Mipsie won 'first go'. Next morning she declared that the Red Sultan had indeed appeared, but her description of him was so vague that a sceptic might have thought she had dreamed the whole thing, but for one curious circumstance. A thick, strongly-scented ash was found on the carpet afterwards, some-what reminiscent of cigar ash, but doubtless emanating from the ghostly hookah. So I think there can be no doubt but that my sister really did receive a visitation that night.

VIII

SABLES AND A STARVED SOUL

THERE is many a lonely heart beating beneath a diamond parure. Golden lorgnettes may conceal tear-dimmed eyes. Underneath a chinchilla rug white hands may clench till their knuckles shine like knuckle-bones in the effort of self-control over some slight, some wounding hurt. . . . This was my poor sister's fate in those early days, when all the world seemed to smile on her and only her intimates knew that Life for her was a hollow mockery.

In those days, of course, an unhappy marriage was screened from the prying eyes of Society by a dignified façade, instead of being paraded before the whole world as it is to-day. For twenty years poor Blousie Banting, (Lady Louise Banting), wore heavy oriental bracelets to conceal the cruel bruises which her husband made by gripping her wrists because—although a brave man in other directions—he was terrified of going upstairs to bed. Lord and Lady Slough of Despond never spoke to each other after their honeymoon, yet the little notes which they wrote to each other on household matters were models of old-world courtesy and always written on the best note-paper. Nowadays what a change do we see! 'How I do dislike my husband,' a young married peeress, who had better be nameless, said to Addle at a dinner party shortly before the war. My husband, unable to believe his ears, thought she must be talking of dustbins and replied: 'Smelly things, I believe'—a remark which puzzled her exceedingly. But to return to Mipsie.

I only wish I could have helped her more during those difficult times, but I myself married before long and was naturally absorbed in my own happy home. Addle too, though the soul of chivalry as a rule, somehow lacked a finer perception of my sister's rare character. I remember recounting to him how I had found Mipsie in tears one day over one of Oxo's typical acts of brutal, freakish humour. She had, the previous week, suddenly realized that she could not meet all her bills out of her allowance, which, though adequate, had its limits, unfortunately. Punctilious to a fault, she had immediately passed them on to her husband, but, in order to soften the slight shock they might cause (for the total was a big one), she packed them in an empty cigar box of his favourite brand and sent it through the post. Oxo said nothing, much to Mipsie's relief, which changed to joy and gratitude the following day when she found on the hall table a package addressed to her in her husband's handwriting, containing—a morocco tiara case! Eagerly she unfastened the catch, only to find an empty case stuffed with the receipted bills. Her bitter disappointment may well be imagined. Yet Addle, when he had heard the piteous story, only remarked 'Good chap, Briskett', and changed the subject. How loyal men are to each other and how insensitive are the best of them to these little barbs that pierce the gentler sex.

Mipsie found consolation in intellectual and artistic interests, and especially in helping on young adventurers in both fields. 'Another of Mipsie's musical pursuits,' I once heard Oxo mutter, when my sister had sprung up and impulsively followed from the room a handsome and talented violinist who had just played exquisitely at a soirée. 'What do you want with these fiddlers?' he asked crossly when she returned. 'Fiddling is better than nothing,' replied Mipsie simply. But I happened to glance down at her lap. She was tearing a delicate seed pearl rope into a thousand shreds.

Thus life continued, inwardly so sad, outwardly so gay. Who will ever forget the Chine House receptions, where ambassadors fought with premiers for ices, and even Royalty lost hairpins, if nothing worse, in the crush? Mipsie's cotillions were always the gayest in London, her favours the most lavishly bestowed. A minor war was started because a certain potentate put his empty plate down on a neighbouring Begum's bare shoulder, mistaking it for a mahogany slab. A long political quarrel was healed when the two statesmen concerned found themselves wedged for a whole evening between a marble Diana and her stag. Mipsie herself was a dominating influence in politics and the confidante of many great men. 'Will there be war, Lord Salisbury?' she boldly asked the premier at the time of the Boer troubles. 'I sincerely hope not, Duchess,' he replied, 'but it is an event that must always be considered a possibility.' Such frankness at such a time shows his trust and high opinion of my sister.

Speaking of foresight over wars reminds me of a delightful story of my dear husband, which I cannot resist telling in conclusion. During the Munich crisis Addle, who is one of the most far-seeing men I know, suddenly realized that the European situation was far from calm, and with that thought he began to worry whether his beloved country was fully prepared for the event of war. He conceived the wise and splendid plan that there should be some form of officers' training corps at public schools, so that the boys who were the future upholders of our race should learn, as he put it simply, 'to hold a rifle like a gentleman.' He spent many months in working out the whole scheme, which he proposed to put to the Lords when completed, and actually got as far as going over to Eton, his old school, to consult the headmaster on the subject. It entailed missing his afternoon nap, but Addle is not the man to shrink from duty. At Eton however, he discovered to his amazement that there is actually a system installed on very similar lines at every public school, only it had slipped his memory. Furthermore, a school contemporary of his whom he happened to meet, taking his great grandson to Rowlands, reminded Addle that he himself had been in the shooting eight one year, when Eton had won the Ashburton Shield. But the lofty idea and the work the scheme entailed remain the same, even though others had thought of it before. It is just another case of 'great minds thinking alike'.

IX

THE FINAL RIFT

WHAT can be more despicable than *noblesse* which does not *oblige*, a duke with the soul of a commoner, a coronet with balls of clay? These epithets—and worse if there be any—might well be showered on my brother-in-law, Oxo Briskett, for refusing the common courtesy of giving grounds for divorce (on the futile plea that the only grounds he knew were those of his own park) and subjecting my poor sister to that humiliation instead. I will spare my dear readers the bitter details, for I have already told the whole sad story in my first book *Lady Addle Remembers*. Suffice it to say that Mipsie found herself in 1903 alone, stripped of everything, including her good name and her pearls, robbed of her children except for six months of the year, struggling to keep body and soul together on the pittance of £3,000 a year which Oxo allowed her. 'I feel outlawed,' she wrote to me from her suite at the Crillon during the first months. My immediate reply was to beg her to leave Paris and make her home with us at Bengers. She accepted gratefully. 'All that I want is to be quiet and to get to know which are my own children,' I remember her saying when she arrived.

Her delightful pair—Ferdy and Millie—were slightly older than my two toddlers, James and Hector, but the four were as devoted as cousins can be, and except for Ferdy trying to drown James—but only in fun—and Millie (an adorable little imp, the image of Mipsie) tying

39

up Heccy with skipping ropes one day and hitting him
in the face with stinging nettles until he gave her his pearl
horse-shoe pin, they were as happy as the day was long.
I was upset with Millie for that episode I must confess,
and I recollect insisting to her mother that the child
must either give Heccy back his pin or be punished.
Mipsie was adamant. 'There is no question about
which course is right,' she said firmly. 'Millie must
be punished.'

Nowadays, of course, the upbringing of children has
greatly changed, and I dare say we should be considered
old fashioned in our methods. My dear Margaret, who
now has the happiest reasons for studying child psychology
writes to me that she is very interested in a new theory
called, apparently, 'Inverted Sin'. I don't really understand it very well but I fancy the idea is that all childish
naughtiness is in reality moral qualities trying to find self-
fulfilment. Thus, breaking things is the unconscious
desire to break down social barriers, telling lies is the
imagination seeking an outlet for expression, bullying
and unkindness is the ego searching for self-reliance, and
greed is just generosity 'beginning at home'. So the
child is encouraged to bully and lie, is given something
new to break each day and supplied with plentiful opportunities for over-eating. In that way the real self is not
repressed and grows out of the cocoon of a disagreeable
child into a fine man or woman. Though there are, I
understand, fairly frequent cases where the early training
takes a hold and is not discarded in later years.

It all seems a trifle too modern to me, but anyway I
am sure I shall love my grandchild, however my dear
Margaret decides as to his or her future upbringing.

But to return to Mipsie and her sojourn at Bengers.
Happy as this was it was not long before she began, very
naturally, to long for 'some tiny corner of my own to

call home,' as she touchingly put it, and she took, as a little *pied-à-terre*, a house in Park Lane, furnishing it entirely from Bengers, 'so'—she expressed it—'as to have something tangible to remember her dear sanctuary by.' I thought this such a beautiful idea, and was also glad in her straightened circumstances to be able to help her in a small way financially, but I was never absolutely certain that Addle saw it in quite the same light. 'How long is Mipsie staying with us?' he asked once during the transition stage between town and country. When I said: 'For as long as she wants to, I hope. Why?' my husband replied: 'I was wondering if we'd have anything left to sit on soon.' This referred, I guessed, to the fact that my boudoir, where we were sitting at the time, was indeed rather chair-less, because Mipsie had lost her heart to the Heppelwhite set which had been there, and the new set I had ordered to replace them had not yet been delivered. I had tried to make things look better by having some packing-cases moved up and draping them with *petit point*, but I fear Addle, who was sitting on one, may have noticed the difference. So in some trepidation I asked 'You do like Mipsie, don't you, dear?' and went on to tell him that only that morning I had had a letter from Oxo in which even he referred to Mipsie's 'taking ways.' My husband smiled and nodded. 'Taking ways is just the right description,' he said, and I felt happy again, realizing that he, too, was a victim to my sister's ineffable charm.

But Mipsie was destined never to dwell in that little Mayfair nest. The reason for her change of plans was a sermon we heard in Great Bengers church from a visiting missionary, just back from India. He discoursed on the great contrast that existed between the poor outcastes among India's teeming millions and the immensely rich Princes, in their palaces like abodes from the Arabian

Nights. Mipsie listened, her eyes gleaming with sympathy for the untouchables, and after the service she sought me in my bedroom.

'Blanchie,' she said, 'I have been wrong in thinking in such a small circumscribed way, when there is so much to see, so many of the world's treasures for all to share. I am going to India, where the thought of such wrongful distribution of wealth haunts me. Perhaps—who knows —I can help to even out those cruel inequalities.'

Within a week she had sold the Park Lane house with all its contents so as to pay for the journey which, as my dear readers will soon see, extended far beyond India. She was thus one of the first cultured women (by which of course I mean English women) to go, alone and unprotected, into the far corners of the globe. Did I say unprotected? No, for such was the appeal of her beauty, her courage, her very helplessness, that wherever she went protectors seemed to spring up, as if by magic, at her side.

X

PASTURES NEW

MIPSIE'S Indian tour started off in the most dramatic manner, as things have a way of doing in her vivid and colourful life, I have noticed. She had scarcely reached India's shores when a message arrived from the all powerful Rajah of Badsore, begging her to accept the use of his motor throughout her visit. It was in the early days of motoring when cars were very liable to break down, so the vehicle was accompanied by a huge royal elephant, richly caparisoned and bearing a jewelled howdah, who lumbered behind the car at the then daring pace of fifteen miles an hour. It was a wise precaution. For in going up a steep incline the car suddenly jibbed—then to the horror of the accompanying train of servants, commenced to run back right into the elephant's hairy chest! Mipsie was quite unperturbed. 'An elephant's chest is a welcome change after my husband,' she records in the journal which she kept throughout the tour. A moment later she felt herself being reverently lifted up by the noble beast and deposited in the howdah, none the worse except for the loss of her motor veil, which he ate. 'Evidently,' she adds, 'an elephant never forgets the British aristocracy.'

The Rajah's A.D.C. apologized humbly for the veil's disappearance and promised that his royal master would present her with another. So touched was Mipsie by this that she immediately descended and offered the elephant her gloves and dustcoat. All three articles were subsequently replaced—and the best that money could buy of course—by His Highness.

Soon she arrived at the fabulous saffron palace, which is now well known to tourists. Tier upon tier of bright yellow marble turrets towered high above the town of Badsore, while all the rugs, furniture and curtains were of the same tint, which is the royal colour and therefore cultivated by tradition to such an extent that the women in the Zenana all wear yellow *saris* and tint their eyelids, etc., with saffron. There was a story that an English girl, staying in the neighbourhood, was once stricken with jaundice. The Rajah happened to see her—had her kidnapped and—so great was his admiration—even contemplated marrying her. Time passed, however, and the girl recovered. The Rajah, in disgust, had her thrown off a 500-foot parapet to some starving jackals, after which unhappy incident I believe she died.

Unfortunately, at the time of Mipsie's visit, the Rajah was in failing health from saffron poisoning, so my sister was only able to see him once. He had been a man of vast appetite, but was on a diet of not more than eight chickens and one pea-hen a day. As he ate the yellow flesh—for they were of course cooked in saffron—Mipsie was fascinated to see him throw the bones over his shoulder out of a window. On asking H. H. the reason for this he told her that his people waited below for anything he had touched, which was considered sacred. Fearing that she might suffer the same fate, Mipsie quickly said: 'I should be honoured if your Highness would also present me with a keepsake.' For answer the Rajah held out his hand. 'Take this,' he said. 'Men have died to gain it'—and he handed her a pea-hen's eye. Only Mipsie's ready wit saved her from having to accept the unpleasant object. 'I regret, your Highness,' she said, 'that my religion forbids me certain parts of pea-hens.'

The Rajah respected her code and presented her with a magnificent yellow emerald instead.

Mipsie went on to stay—in great contrast to the Rajah of Badsore—with the gentle and cultured Marharaj Rana of Singhit Bunji, who, born of a warrior race in which every prince of the blood had, on attaining his fifteenth birthday, to prove his merit by killing 50 tigers, 50 leopards and either 100 sambur or 200 natives, revolted against this butchery, became a Christian, and a vegetarian and joined the R.S.P.C.A. Subsequently he made a law in his province that no one should take life. This had its disadvantages as, of course, even vermin was preserved, and the fleas wore gold collars and were encouraged to enjoy a good meal from high and low alike. The Marharaj Rana achieved wonders in the taming of beasts of prey and he invited Mipsie to go and see his favourite tiger who he was slowly converting to vegetarianism by placing near its lair exquisite silver dishes containing peaches, asparagus and cream cakes. The only thing that caused the animal to revert to type was, apparently, the sight of another tiger or other creature of prey.

Unfortunately the experiment proved a failure that time, as for some unaccountable reason the moment the tiger set eyes on Mipsie he began to snarl and roar, and so had to be driven away by the servants, leaving untouched a beautiful *ommelette aux fines herbes* and a *pêche Melba*.

Space forbids that I should describe the whole of Mipsie's Indian tour. There was the wonderful aviary palace of Hotgong, filled with birds of every species and hue, including the sacred parrots which were trained to screech every time the Newab of Hotgong approached. Mipsie said they made a fearful clamour, especially during the night. Then there was the Rajah of Ahgotodabad, with whom she stayed longest, whose fairy tale jewels extended even to the furniture. Mipsie had a vast bath mat, she says—too big to go into her trunk, (she tried)—encrusted round the border with precious stones of the first grade. On another occasion there was an amusing episode when her host had a visitor of equal rank staying with him, and as a matter of etiquette it was impossible to decide with whom an English duchess should go in to dinner. Mipsie solved it by sitting on the shoulders of one with her hands clasping the osprey on the other's turban (the osprey came off in her hands!). A very neat solution I think.

Eventually her tour came to an end. 'I am the richer by some wonderful experiences,' she wrote in her journal, 'but still I feel that the world is an oyster which has not really yielded me up its pearl,' and with that ideal in mind she decided to return to England via Arabia and Egypt, of which I shall write in the next chapter.

XI

FROM RED SEA TO BLACK TREACHERY

AT Aden Mipsie left the comparative comfort of her luxury liner and boldly embarked, entirely alone save for her secretary and courier, Major Hardup, her personal maid, and the captain and little crew of twenty, on the beautiful steam yacht which had been lent to her by a friend for the remainder of her trip.

Their first objective was Uassa Land, that picturesque little colony just above Eritrea which is ruled over by a line of Merchant Princes whose traditional generosity is only equalled by their devotion to England. It was these splendid qualities which appealed to my sister and which prompted her to ask Major Hardup, whom she met on the boat, and who had had considerable experience in native parts, to arrange the tour for her. He gladly accepted, enchained by her beauty at once, and also most grateful for the generous remuneration which she offered him, for he was on half pay with no private money, poor man. It is terrible to think there are such cases of hardship amongst British officers.

Mipsie's vivid journal describes their journey from Port Maggot on the Red Sea, up the famous Red Mite gorges to Nojoko, the capital.

'The sun rises here at four o'clock, spreading deep crimson and purple lights over the rocks, an unforgettable sight, the description of which made a deep impression on me as Major Hardup gave it at breakfast on my *crumpet* (hotel verandah) five hours later. I hastily swallowed coffee and *jim-jams* (native rolls) and caught the only train in the day, which leaves at ten a.m. As it is too hot to travel after ten-thirty we left the train at Badeg and waited for our *skivvi-bog* (procession of servants on donkeys) to catch up with us. All round us were wonderful flowering eggs, while brilliant yellow flying adders zoomed overhead. 'They are attracted by your face powder,' Major Hardup explained, 'but are quite harmless.'

'The natives will trade anything for toothpicks. We brought several thousand with us and purchased a good supply of *nitties*—a kind of banana-shaped pineapple, and plentiful *oompahs*—a delicious pineapple, looking and tasting exactly like a banana. Also emu's eggs and several bottles of *tjck*—the native fiery wine which the better caste tribes drink before killing their grandmothers, a regular custom on Friday nights at sundown. At Skrewi we were fortunate enough to see a native wedding, which was most interesting. The bride is entirely swathed in pampas gauze, while the bridegroom is clothed only in gourds, which are hung round him in such profusion that he can hardly move. While the villagers beat the *chummi* (a rude kind of gong) the local maidens slowly unwind the veiling and the bridegroom's friends, in a kind of leaping dance, remove his gourds one by one. It was thrilling to watch, and I found myself longing to take part, but Major Hardup said it would be a riot so firmly removed me, alas, before the ceremony was completed. I was told that the bride is usually so scratched by the pampas gauze and the bridegroom so bruised by the gourds that they are frequently unable to meet again for weeks. Divorce is very prevalent in Uassa land.'

At Nojoko Mipsie was met by Ras Bollinogud's servants and conducted with great ceremony to his palace. Here a

MIPSIE IN UASSA-LAND NATIVE COSTUME

bitter disappointment awaited her. Ever since she had
arrived in Uassa she had been under the protection of the
Prince, who had frequently intimated, in letters and
through his agents, that a gift worthy of an English
duchess awaited her at the capital. On the palace steps
she was handed a paper listing 'the gift': '200 fat black
sheep, 100 *yonghi* (the local blue oxen, born mad, considered a great delicacy eaten raw), 50 alligators' hides,
1 cwt. of incense and 10 jars of snake oil.' It was, from
Ras Bollinogud's viewpoint, doubtless the most generous
present, but to my sister it was naturally a blow, having
expected something more portable and utilitarian, like
precious stones or gold. However, with her unfailing
good manners she thanked the Prince for his favour—
then, with one of her impetuous gestures of reckless generosity, she turned to Major Hardup. 'These are for you,'
she said in French. 'Your salary for the trip.' So
overcome was her secretary by the gift—which was, of
course, worth many times his due—that he had to sit
down and ask for brandy. Indeed, he did not completely recover his equilibrium till they had left Nojoko
and were on their return journey to Port Maggot. Then
suddenly, while sipping their coffee outside a little *bumbar*
(very homely estaminet) he surprised Mipsie by springing
to his feet and exclaiming, with fear in his eyes as he spoke
the words:

'We must get to the coast as soon as possible. Ras
Bollinogud will be furious at our leaving his gifts behind.
which is considered a grave insult to a host. We are in
great danger.'

The warning of Ras Bollinogud's treachery came too
late. When Mipsie turned her horrified gaze to the little
village square behind her it was to see a crowd of natives
approaching, their *pokos* (four-edged spears) gleaming in
the sunlight, murder in their faces.

It was a terrible moment. Major Hardup, who to do him justice was ready to pay for his unforgivable lapse with his life, immediately sprang to Mipsie's side. But where blood is blue hearts are stout. She pushed him impatiently aside and standing to her full height, faced the angry people, holding in her hand an empty envelope.

'I have here,' she said in clarion tones, 'a letter to our Foreign Secretary, Sir Edward Grey. Beside me'—and she pointed with a firm hand)—'is a pillar box. Unless you go quietly to your homes I shall post this letter, and in less than two months the entire British Army will come to my aid, and you and your wives and children will be annihilated.'

The threat worked. The fire died out of their eyes and there was a great hush over the square. Then suddenly, a handsome young Uassan sprang up beside Mipsie.

'Three cheers for the Duchess and the British Foreign Office,' he shouted—and the little town rang with loyal cries.

Thus was the situation saved by a woman's courage and the world-wide respect commanded by the British aristocracy and the British Constitution.

XII

SLAVES OF DESTINY

WITH all her amazing beauty and charm, Mipsie is also far better educated than nineteen peeresses out of twenty. Thus it was that she had heard of the 'Thousand and One Nights,' and was determined to experience their delights for herself. Major Hardup, who of course knew the Arabians from end to end, eagerly agreed to conduct her once more.

Accordingly they landed at el Bismuth and proceeded by camel to the busy little town of Hamfist, famous for its dyes (which are made from crushed spiders, these insects being of every hue and as big as tennis balls). Mipsie and Major Hardup explored the market the first day and my sister was entranced by the brilliantly coloured costumes and draperies she saw and bought for herself a beautiful royal blue and jade green dress, heavily embroidered in gold beads, together with a pearl pink yashmak. These she donned next day, and delighted her secretary by giving him an imitation of an oriental dance on her wash-hand-stand! Then, much to his alarm, she announced her firm intention of sallying forth into the streets thus attired. He tried to dissuade her, but in vain, and all he could do was to follow her at a distance. Perhaps he had some premonition of the dreadful fate that awaited her?

For a time all went well. Mipsie threaded her way into the busy market-place un-noticed. Then suddenly she found herself in a ring of women, all dressed, as she was, in peasant finery, while there appeared to be some kind of auction in process, with a good deal of shouting and arguing in many strange tongues. Meanwhile, poor Major Hardup had quite lost sight of her amidst the thronging crowd. Time passed and he became more and more worried, so much so indeed that he had to return to their hotel and ask for brandy. His search continued far into the evening, until he had explored every corner of Hamfist and every restorative the town possessed. Eventually, from various sources, he pieced together the terrible history. A particularly powerful sheikh, Abdul Akrid bin Sniftah, had that day descended from his mountain castle and purchased a large consignment of female slaves, who had already been conveyed into captivity by bullock carts (though we learnt later that Mipsie had ridden on Abdul's own camel, the sheikh walking beside her). Major Hardup groaned aloud as he staggered into the hotel bar when the fearful truth broke upon him.

Mipsie had been sold into slavery.

What were our feelings when we received his cable I leave my dear readers to imagine. Even Addle, who seldom shows emotion, had no heart to shoot that day and spent the morning scratching his favourite pig's back and thinking of Mipsie in the sheikh's power. The awful part was that we could do nothing. Major Hardup had indicated that he was trying to redeem Mipsie by purchasing goats, which was the exchange most appreciated by a sheikh. But beyond cabling 'Buy to the limit,' we could only wait for news. When it came it seemed the end of hope. Major Hardup had offered 1,000 goats—an enormous price—but Abdul bin Sniftah flatly refused to part with my sister.

It is in such black moments that inspiration sometimes comes to pierce the gloom. Suddenly I saw clearly the only possible solution; my family's famous breed of Balder goats must be sacrificed. My father was unfortunately on one of his business trips in Paris, so Addle went post-haste to Coots Balder, empowered by him to give the word—which my brother Crainy[1], who was very seldom heard to speak at all, would find it almost impossible to utter—that would send out to Arabia as many of our beloved goats as might be necessary to buy my sister's freedom—ten, twenty, one hundred if need be. To our unutterable relief a cable came from the sheikh himself, after he had received a minute description of the goats, saying that he would release Mipsie in exhange for two. 'One woman is much the same as another but a new breed of goats is an occasion,' he is reported to have said— hardly a gallant remark, but we were all too overjoyed to cavil.

It was sad that Major Hardup was laid low with alco-holic malaria and could not go himself to conduct my sister back—doubly sad as it transpired, in that he sent as a deputy a friend of his Sandhurst days, Sir Constant Standing, who was in Arabia for the scorpion shooting. He immediately fell a victim to Mipsie's beauty, clearly visible even through her now torn garments, and she in her turn was attracted to him, for it was many weeks since she had seen a white man. Besides, Constant was undoubtedly good looking as well as being a fine soldier and a baronet of an old family. Noting that he seemed occasionally pre-occupied and worried, Mipsie, with her quick sympathy, soon drew him out and learnt that he was indeed concerned at the moment by the hourly expected death of his uncle, the enormously rich Lord Parsimony, who had declared him his heir. Pity, they say, is akin to love. Perhaps it was

[1] Viscount Crainiham.

this womanly emotion, perhaps it was relief at her freedom, or perhaps it was just Destiny, that had once made
a slave of my sister and was now to cast her into the far
more bitter slavery of a second unhappy marriage. However it may be, it was as Lady Millicent Standing that
Mipsie embarked, after a primitive six weeks' honeymoon
at Shepherd's Hotel, Cairo, to return to England and
Home--she brought the Beauty with her.

XIII

A NEW INTEREST

As so often happens in life, the very strength and fervour of Mipsie's sympathy with her new husband over the grave illness of his millionaire uncle, Lord Parsimony, wore her out and made the old man's sudden recovery seem somehow like an anti-climax in which she was incapable of showing or even feeling any joy. In addition, it is well known that Lord Parsimony was a puritan of the deepest dye, who rigidly disapproved of divorce and consequently of his nephew's beautiful wife. In fact, Mipsie strongly suspected him of rallying simply in order to upset her, which would have been base and unkind behaviour indeed. However this may be, she felt sadly depressed and disillusioned on her return to England— a depression which was increased by many bitter letters from Major Hardup, still laid up in Hamfist, in which he accused her of discarding him like an old love. To counteract the effect of these sad episodes she decided on a few months in the South of France, as a mental pick-me-up for her and perhaps a financial pick-me-up for her husband, whose fortunes were very low after his uncle's unexpected recovery. 'Besides,' Mipsie said when she told me of the plan, 'Constant is such a keen sportsman. The pigeon-shooting will make up for his disappointment at missing his partridges this year.' I recount this little anecdote so that my dear readers may see that Mipsie at any rate intended to 'love, honour and cherish' in her second marriage.

It cannot be denied that gambling is in every Coot's blood. There are, indeed, many instances of this passion leading my family to strange and even desperate passes. The fourth Earl, in 1730, once played faro for five days and nights on end. When eventually he won a fortune from his opponent and essayed to rise—he could not move. His beard had grown round one of his own legs! On another occasion the Viscount Crainiham of the time, having wagered everything to another young blood (except Coots Balder, which was entailed), had nothing left to offer except his aunt, Lady Emily Coot, who was refused as being too old and ugly. When it was pointed out that she was possessed of a fortune amounting to five figures, the gambler wittily said: 'It's her own figure I object to.' However, he accepted the wager, which he won. He was then in a quandary as to how to take possession of a bed-ridden old lady of eighty-seven. Eventually he had her kidnapped (including her bed), and set about investigating her will. He found that Lady Emily, herself an inveterate gambler, had lost the whole of her fortune a few days previously to another octogenarian in a contest of who could turn round in bed the greatest number of times in an hour.

But to return to Mipsie. She and Constant settled down very happily at Monte Carlo, and for a time I hoped that their mutual interest of the tables—not that he was so keen on gambling—would draw them together into the serenity of a happy English family life. I confess that I did not greatly enjoy our only visit to them. Addle missed his pigs sorely, and caused rather an upset at the Casino by asking for the windows to be opened, and I kept on worrying about how the village would get on without me. But it is always an interesting experience to glance into a world outside one's own, and I was able to give a nice little talk on Monte Carlo to my Mothers'

Union when I returned—only fearing that the mention of gambling might have a harmful effect on their quiet lives, I pretended that nothing but halma was played— an innocent little deception which I hope my recording angel will forgive.

For a long time Mipsie's luck at the tables was amazing, and the talk of Monaco. Indeed, visitors seated round the roulette board used to hail my sister's entrance into the *salon* with delight and implore her to come and sit on them so as to bring them fortune. In one year she amassed over 200,000 francs, bought herself a string of pearls and allowed Constant to give her an ermine wrap. Then suddenly, fickle fortune changed and they had to see most of their gains disappear. Constant's ineptness, his inherent weakness of character now showed itself. Mipsie had done her share—it was obviously his turn to come to their rescue and make money, as she justly pointed out. Instead, he only continued to lose. 'You have no backbone, no system in life,' Mipsie told him with some bitterness. As a result, he spent much time on working out several systems which eventually led them both to disaster, as the following chapter will show.

I must end on a happier note—an amusing story of how Mipsie once acted as a pawnbroker! One day, on the terrace near the Casino, she chanced to see a young girl in tears, while a very handsome young man was endeavouring to comfort her. Mipsie, with her ready sympathy, immediately asked the cause. It was the same old story —they had lost every penny on their honeymoon and could not even pay their hotel bill. 'If only I could get back to Austria,' the girl wept, 'my father never denies me anything. But we haven't even the fare.' Mipsie patted her arm. 'Don't worry, my child,' she said soothingly. 'I will pay your fare for you.' The girl gasped: 'Madame! Will you really trust me?' Mipsie smiled her most roguish smile. 'No, my dear,' she said, 'but my husband will escort you to Austria and back and you shall leave your husband with me as security till you return.' Surely the most curious transaction that can ever have taken place in that romantic little Principality, but one that indeed testifies to my sister's warm and all-embracing heart.

XIV

FORTUNE'S WHEEL

CONSTANT was unfortunately no mathematician, and he would have been far wiser to admit frankly to this failing instead of attempting to work out systems for roulette and baccarat which were quite beyond his mental powers, and cost Mipsie thousands of francs in testing. It also meant a time of great loneliness for my poor sister, who would sally forth by herself each day after locking her husband into his room as a gentle encouragement to work.

During these months of enforced widowhood many strange and dramatic things happened to her, as is ever the way in her vivid life. One evening she was walking through the casino gardens when a certain Russian nobleman, a few yards ahead, drew his revolver and placed it to his temple! She was just in time to strike his hand away, so that the bullet sped harmlessly into a passing peasant. In gratitude, he gave her his magnificent sable-lined cape before taking prussic acid. On another occasion she became involved—innocently of course—in a daring plot to rob the casino. A rich Cuban had recently arrived in his luxury yacht and had aroused the interest of the whole of Monaco by his dark handsome features and flashing eyes, as well as by his strange, somewhat unusual habits, such as picking his teeth with a jewelled dagger. Mipsie, always fascinated by the bizarre, was equally keen to meet the stranger, but no one seemed able to effect an introduction. But my sister is nothing if not unconventional and impulsive—she once achieved acquaintanceship with a famous 'cellist by throwing herself at his feet and embracing his instrument—and she determined not to be beaten in this instance. Accordingly, she smuggled herself on board his yacht disguised as a great sheaf of madonna lilies, and thus attired posed on the dining table at a party which transpired to be entirely composed of men. To her astonishment, as the dinner proceeded, she heard discussed every detail of a daring plot to rob the *salle privée*. The only thing missing, apparently, was some one of irreproachable social standing, to give the gang the entrée to that millionaires' haven. Such was Mipsie's excitement at these words that several madonnas trembled and fell off her. The company, seeing what was beneath the snow-white petals, rose as one man, as the Cuban handed her down from the table and filled her to the brim with champagne.

'Gentlemen,' said Mipsie to gain time, 'I am at your disposal.'

Somehow or other the casino administration got wind of the plot, however, before Mipsie could warn them. The Cuban and his accomplices left Monaco as suddenly as they arrived and were never seen again. The curious thing is that when the former, in a rage, demanded who had betrayed them, the Chef de Sûreté replied enigmatically: 'Nobody, M'sieur. Our suspicions were aroused by the company you keep'—a remark that remains a mystery to this day. But when Mipsie sought an interview with the casino authorities and told them that she had intended to inform on the gang that very day, they only smiled and bowed her out. No large reward, as is customary when a fraud is exposed. Such is official gratitude.

After that, things went from bad to worse with Constant and my poor sister, who were often hard put to it to know where their next *mille* was coming from. Then suddenly, fortune's wheel turned once more. Constant, who was decidedly clever with his hands, had made himself a roulette wheel on which to test his systems. It was so much admired that there was quite a demand from their many friends for roulette wheels for private parties. Of course, not being an expert, it was impossible to make them absolutely true, but as Mipsie told him, that only added to their charm, like crazy beams in an old house (she has often told me how she loves anything crooked) and she also encouraged him to paint each one slightly differently, so as to give them distinction. Orders poured in, and things began to look up a little for Mipsie as with the money Constant made she played carefully and astutely at private parties only—for the casino had somewhat lost its charm since a system they had tried called the *coup de poivre*—which involved making the croupier sneeze at a certain point, I believe—had seemed in some way to annoy the management, who being foreigners had, of course, no sense of humour.

Then, without warning, the blow fell.

Mipsie had just broken the bank on one of Constant's wheels at a private party given by a Grand Duke, when to the astonishment of all, an American woman, who had lost heavily, accused my sister of playing on inside knowledge of the wheel.

Mipsie, like any loyal wife, appealed to her husband.

'Constant,' she demanded, 'are you going to sit there and hear me insulted?'

The incredible, the unforgivable thing then happened. *Constant said 'Yes.'*

She left him next day and came, like a wounded bird, to Bengers. Even so she might have returned to him, for he wrote her a letter of abject apology, saying that he was so used to agreeing with her over everything that the words had automatically slipped out. But while she was considering what was best to do his uncle, Lord Parsimony, died and cut his nephew out of his will entirely. Mipsie felt that he must have had good cause, to take such a drastic step, since before his marriage to Mipsie Lord Parsimony had always declared his nephew to be his heir. 'If only I had known that he was really worthless I would never have married him,' poor Mipsie said bitterly, when I gave her the cheque for her divorce expenses, which her husband was unable to pay.

Constant has continued to go downhill, I fear. He lived on in the South of France, where a friend of Addle's saw him just before the war, clad only in old flannel trousers with nothing above them. 'What's happened to your shirt, Constant?' called out our friend. Constant's reply, in execrable taste, shows the depth of his descent. 'I put it on the wrong wife,' he is said to have answered.

XV

THE STRUGGLE FOR EXISTENCE

In 1908 Mipsie's chief problem was that of finance. Indeed this might be said to apply to almost every year of her brave, romantic life. Her pin-money of £3,000 a year from Briskett nowhere near sufficed to meet her commitments, and she had nothing else to fall back on, except her jewels, of which she gallantly refused to sell so much as one hatpin. I remember Addle coming upon her one day at Bengers (where she always lives in between husbands) laying out her collection on a stool for my benefit. 'Those your frozen assets, Mipsie?' he asked. My sister laughingly shook her head. 'My assets are never frozen,' she replied.

In those days, of course, no woman of the *beau monde* ever dreamed of earning her living, and indeed I strongly deprecate the custom which heavy taxation has forced upon us to-day. I shall never forget how shocked I was when an old friend of mine, Craggie Kruschen (Baroness Kruschen, a cousin of the Hapsburgs) came to see me a few years ago, saying she was on her way to work. 'What work?' I inquired. 'Oh, charring,' was the gay reply. 'I go every day and scrub for Pamela Pershore and she does the same for me. Our servants wouldn't respect us if we did our own houses.' As a matter of fact, Craggie had the best of the bargain, because the Duchess of Pershore's house was always a centre of Society, so she was able to write something called a gossip column, very lucrative apparently, on the strength of what she learned below-stairs.

But to return to Mipsie. One day, after reading an article in the *Queen* on the subject of American admiration of English Society, she bethought her of inserting an advertisement in a famous daily paper, graciously offering her help to American parents in launching their daughters. The response was overwhelming—so much so that she was able to pick and choose, and true to her ideals select only those families who loved their daughters so deeply that money was no object where their welfare was concerned. Her prospectus read as follows:

Minimum charge per season per daughter   .   £500
With Court Presentation (this to include private
    dances, Ranelagh, Lords, etc. Court and
    special balls, Ascot, Box at Opera and personal
    contact with Royalty extra)   .   .   .   £750

MARRIAGE TERMS.

English Duke £2,000
Ditto Marquess or Earl £1,500
Ditto, Viscount, Baron or Baronet .   . from £1,000
Foreign Royalty or title   .   By arrangement
Financier   .   . 2½ per cent on Bridegroom's income
REDUCTIONS are allowed in the event of marriages with clergy, penniless Lieutenant, schoolmaster, country doctor, etc.

Mipsie had a very successful first season with this new venture, taking on two delightful girls at the full rate. Indeed, she was forced to charge more for one, pointing out to her parents that she had a slight squint and that marriage would therefore be more difficult to arrange, but her devoted father, Mr. Quiston B. Grape, was only too ready to pay the extra, and the result was a happy alliance with a new peer, in which Mipsie got the commission for a baron and also 2½ per cent on his income, as she justly claimed that he would never have been given his title but for his generous contributions to party funds and that therefore he ranked as a financier. The other girl, pretty Mamie Druggett, was not quite so easy. The business started off badly by her having a great success at a dance with what she styled 'a real English Dooke'. Mipsie, who had been playing bridge downstairs and unfortunately lost, was too distracted to inquire his name, but cheered by the possibility of a good marriage for her young protégé, begged Mamie to invite him to dinner next day. When he arrived it transpired to be Oxo! Of course, with his brutal directness, he declared that nothing would induce him to handle anything sponsored by his former wife, and the disconsolate girl had to see her beau depart. Eventually she fell madly in love with a penniless young naval officer, which caused my sister much worry and many upsetting scenes with the girl, till it was suddenly discovered that that young man was heir to a baronetcy, so all was well and she was awarded her hard-earned commission.

But Fate seems to have decreed that nothing should succeed for long with my poor sister, and the following year saw the end of her valuable social work amongst American débutantes.

She had just married one girl to an Earl, after a slight unpleasantness with her father, who argued that the fee should be £1,500, whereas Mipsie charged £2,000 because he was a Duke's heir. Eventually it was amicably settled by Mipsie threatening to marry the bridegroom herself if she did not get her whole fee. She then had left only Alice McWhittle Potts, daughter of the biscuit king who could well afford more than £2,000. Mipsie looked everywhere for a foreign royalty but there were none available. Eventually, she went to the Balkans, where she had heard that it was easy to pick up Princes cheap at the time. Sure enough, she soon found a young man who declared that for £1,000 he could establish his claim as hereditary Prince of Sofa. Mipsie promised this sum, also marriage with a millionaire's daughter, on consideration of a reasonable income for herself after his wedding. All seemed well—Mr. Potts delighted at the prospect of a Prince, Alice enchanted with her bridegroom. Then a terrible thing happened. The Prince was unfortunately rather a heavy drinker, and when his prospective father-in-law arrived the day before the wedding, he was not entirely sober. Mr. Potts inquired: 'Are you His Highness?' The young man replied: 'I am no more Highness than you, sir, but Lady Millicent knows some old fool who will pay £1,000 for me to call myself Prince.'

The resulting scenes may be imagined! Mr. Potts was furious and said unforgivable things to Mipsie before he took his daughter away. The bridegroom seemed equally incensed and actually expected my sister to pay his debts in England. In the end, he accepted the cheque Addle gave him to return to his own country and the whole miserable affair was settled. But poor Mipsie's nerves were considerably shattered by the episode and I had to present her daughter Millie for her, as she said she felt, after her last experience, she could never touch a débutante again.

XVI

A THIRD DISILLUSIONMENT

AFTER the sadness of her second disillusionment (which word I always employ in Mipsie's case in preference to 'marriage') and her unlucky experiences in a wholly laudable attempt to earn her daily *brioche*, it is not surprising that my sister longed to start afresh, with 'a new country, new friends, new money,' as she expressed it. Accordingly she planned to go to America, in spite of the cruel treatment she had received from the U.S.A. through the person of Mr. McWhittle Potts. But forgiveness has ever been an inherent part of her sweet character, and she was greatly attracted by the stories her young débutantes had told her of that land of plenty of millionaires—stories which made her think that she might at last find a Utopia where there was not the endless stress and struggle for filthy lucre which lays waste our time elsewhere; it would just fall into her lap. She was fascinated too by the romantic tales the girls told her of their homes in New York and Baltimore—the picturesque gold dinner services, the old-world charm of rose diamonds round the porch.

She was just on the eve of departure, and Addle, who thoroughly approved this new step and had indeed even bought her ticket for her, was about to escort her to Liverpool 'so as to be sure she didn't get on the wrong ship and have to come back again,' as he jokingly put it, when Fate once more intervened.

At a soirée at the Russian Embassy she was presented

to Prince Fédor Ubetzkoi, already an old and sick man. These two qualities were quite enough to appeal to my sister's innate womanliness, and when she learnt that he was the ruler of Goulashia, with that beautiful little country solidly behind him—solid with platinum mines, that he was seventy-six and a widower, with a weak heart, her own heart contracted with pain at the thought of the journey she had so nearly taken. 'Do the work that's nearest' was a favourite motto of my beloved mother's, and Mipsie must have recollected it at this moment, for within a week she had cancelled all her plans and as Princess Fédor Ubetzkoi was journeying back with her husband to Ekaterinbog, the capital of Goulashia.

Here the first of her disappointments awaited her.

Fédor can hardly be blamed perhaps for his age, for that very senility which appealed to Mipsie so greatly, but he would have been well advised to have had some young attaché or A.D.C. always at hand to tell strangers what had apparently passed completely from his mind, that he had by a first marriage a daughter of forty, Irina, who ruled like a queen in Ekaterinbog, and a twenty-five year old son Michel, who would of course inherit Goulashia and every grain of platinum in the country.

However, Mipsie was never one to cry over spilt Bristol Milk, and she soon accepted the situation philosophically and looked around for where her next task lay. Immediately she saw her duty clear. Prince Fédor was obviously not long for this world; but Prince Michel was young—the future of Goulashia and everything in it was in his hands. My sister determined that she would join hands with him in this sacred trust.

She was abundantly rewarded. Michel became completely devoted to his stepmother, and for two happy years they were scarcely ever—indeed the maliciously-minded said never—apart. But Mipsie cared not a fig

PRINCE MICHEL UBETSKOI

for gossip and she and 'Mich' just laughed at court disapproval and Irina's frowns. (For some unaccountable reason the Princess seemed against my sister from the first.) They rode, danced and fished in the lake together. They indulged in revolver practice on the palace chickens, a special breed in which Princess Irina took great pride. She begged her father to intervene and he actually put his foot down and insisted that they practice on serfs instead. (Prince Fédor was a great admirer of England, and when he heard that pheasant shooting was a pastime of the landed gentry he determined to adopt it in his own country. Unfortunately, not being a good linguist, he interpreted the phrase as 'peasant shooting' and acted accordingly.) Above all, they took part in private theatricals.

All my family have inherited histrionic ability to a marked degree. My brother Crainy is known as Crambo to this day, so effective was he in dumb parts, while Mipsie was always inimitable as the black sheep when we sang the famous nursery rhyme to visitors. It happened that acting had also been a great tradition at Ekaterinbog Palace, where there was a beautiful little theatre, decorated in sky-blue plush and platinum, each *fauteuil* being fitted with a crystal carafe of vodka and a small revolver, in case a revolution should break out unexpectedly in the middle of a performance. So far, the court had only given the French classics, but Mipsie changed all that as she changed many things in Goulashia. She introduced light opera, musical comedy and even pantomime, playing the principal boy's role herself. To the amazed and scandalized palace set she tried to explain that it was 'an old English custom,' but they were, I fear, too rigid and prejudiced to appreciate this facet of British culture. She received, however, the whole-hearted support of the army, and especially of Prince Fédor's bodyguard, who made Mispie the toast of every regimental dinner, drinking her health in their own top boot and then throwing the boot on the fire, as was the Goulashian custom. The officer who could hop home after the festivities without toppling over was then supposed to win the lady. One day thirty officers hopped home successfully! Poor Mipsie, she never told me how she got out of that quandary, as State affairs kept her too busy to write for several weeks.

Meanwhile, like a snake in the grass, the storm clouds were brewing in Ekaterinbog which were shortly to undermine the silver lining of my sister's happiness.

XVII

REVOLUTION IN GOULASHIA

In my last chapter I told my dear readers how Mipsie introduced many things to her adopted country—good old English customs such as pantomime, brandy and soda, rubber hot-water bottles at the palace, to replace their primitive though picturesque platinum warming-pans, which she had sent home to England instead, as a keepsake. She also persuaded Prince Fédor to alter the New Year tradition of every man and woman saluting their own sex with three kisses, accompanied by the greeting 'St. Plasticine attend thee,' to the same delightful action applied to the opposite sex instead. It was a popular move with the more advanced Students' Party and with the army, but in the rigid Court circles it was considered an innovation. Other things seemed to Mipsie unjust and uncivilized and she threw all the weight of her husband and stepson into a gallant attempt to amend them. For instance, it was customary to pay honour only to unmarried women in Goulashia. On midsummer day the men would always present young girls with gifts, accompanied by a sprig of maidenhair fern, while the married women received nothing, and those who had had more than one husband were forced to shut themselves up all day with their blinds drawn. This struck my sister as positively cruel and while she was in Goulashia she did her utmost to establish the proper position of married women and special recognition of divorcées. In this she had Fédor's full support—indeed he was first attracted

71

to Mipsie because of her late divorce, which he believed to be an integral part of the English Society he admired so greatly—and for Prince Michel of course she could do no wrong. But her stepdaughter Irina thought otherwise, and she, unfortunately, still held sway over a large portion of the population.

The first sign of trouble was a small bomb in Mipsie's muff which she suddenly discovered whilst attending Sunday service in the cathedral. She dropped it in the alms-box and thought no more of the matter. But two days later she found another concealed in a hat which came by post from Paris. It must be explained that in Goulashia revolutions were very frequent, and every peasant was taught to make bombs from childhood. A whole family used to sit round the fire in winter time, Mipsie told me, carving and painting with great skill, bombs of every shape and size. Luckily the Goulashians were very poor mechanics so it was rare for one actually to go off; still, it was a factor that had to be considered, and as chocolate-coated bombs began to appear in a full box of sweets ('my bon-bombs' Mipsie used laughingly to call them) and tiny white bombs in her sugar basin on her breakfast tray, it became necessary for her maid to sample everything first, in case of accidents.

On Easter Sunday, 1910, the storm burst. When Prince Fédor, in accord with an age-old custom, presented each of his bodyguard with a brightly-painted bad egg at the Easter Parade, the men one and all dashed the eggs to the ground, where they broke into a thousand chickens. The same day, slogans began to appear all over Ekaterinbog; '*Przmt copijk Britovzka bgowdl.*' 'Get rid of the British ——' Mipsie said I shouldn't understand the last word even if it were translated. To make things worse, Fédor's ninety-six-year-old mother, Princess Amnesia Ubekskoi, immediately moved back to the palace, saying that she had always been on the spot for every revolution and was not going to alter the habits of a lifetime. She was devoted to Princess Irina, and was consequently another thorn in Mipsie's all-too-tender side.

Even so, it is doubtful if my sister—absorbed in her delightful friendship with Prince Michel—realized fully the seriousness of the situation, until she learnt of the strikes in the platinum mines. Immediately she awoke to the danger that might befall Goulashia, should her staple industry be ruined. Mipsie herself had asked Fédor, on their marriage, for a block of platinum shares, 'so that she could share in the life-blood of her new country' as she beautifully expressed it. She knew, therefore, that the strikes could only bring disaster—bread famine for the people, dividend famine for herself. As ever with her, action followed knowledge.

The Goulashians are an intensely superstitious people, And especially do they revere their patron saint, St. Plasticine, who was actually a reigning prince in the fourteenth century, canonized on account of his liberality to the poor. He is depicted always in white, with flowing golden hair and beard, carrying a jewelled box containing roubles. Mipsie had the brilliant idea of donning her costume for Prince Charming in *Cinderella* and, accompanied by Michel, driving by sleigh round to the various mines, where inflammatory meetings were held most evenings. An arc light, attached to the horse's tail, shone full upon her as she made her stirring appeal, as from their patron saint. The effect was electrical. Some knelt, many wept, all went back to the mines. . . .

Thus did my sister persuade 90 per cent of the strikers to resume work. (What irony, as she said afterwards, that she should persuade men not to 'down tools' when two husbands had done so to her!) But at length there came a day when the welcome was so overpowering that the crowd came too close. One miner inadvertently knocked from Mipsie's hand the jewelled box, associated with the saint, which she always carried. It opened as it fell—and out of it poured sticks of grease-paint, mascara, yards of false hair. The next moment a foreman, his suspicions suddenly aroused, twitched away Mipsie's long golden beard—and a howl of fury went up from the mob : 'It's the English——' (again that word that I shouldn't understand.) Somehow, Michel got Mipsie away to safety, and the discovery was hushed up by all the miners concerned being sent to Siberia. My sister had saved the country—but at what a price! For in the emergency they were forced to abandon the sleigh which they had used throughout the tour—a sleigh in which the whole of the driver's seat had been filled almost to the brim with solid platinum nuggets.

XVIII

C'EST LA GUERRE!

SOON after the romantic happenings of the last chapter, when Mipsie saved Goulashia from the gory fangs of revolution, other troubles descended upon my poor sister which were to make her hate the very name of marriage. Chief among them was the engagement of her stepson, Prince Michel, and the end of the friendship which had perhaps been the happiest part of her life. 'Mich is going to marry that horrible little Xenia Nastikoff,' she wrote despairingly to me in 1911, 'and I, who love every inch of him, am thrust aside, without even a settlement to remember him by.' This tragic betrayal from one to whom she had indeed given amazing devotion for a stepmother, seemed to have the effect of drawing Mipsie closer to her husband, who was now a complete invalid, his mind wandering in a most distressing manner.

Talking of wandering minds recalls a cousin of my mother's, the fifth Duke of Brawling, whose senility took the form of making new and decidedly eccentric wills almost daily, witnessed only by his terrified servants (for he was a violent man). What was his widow's consternation to learn, when eventually the last will was read, that he had left his entire fortune to his horse! She afterwards had cause for rejoicing, however, for the horse soon died too and, having no heirs, the money returned to his benefactor's family, while no death duties were paid either by the horse or the Duchess, because it was found that there were no laws in England relating to death duties for horses.

Some remembrance of this story may have been in Mipsie's mind, however—possibly recalled by Princess Irina's strong resemblance to a horse—which induced her scarcely to leave Prince Fédor's side during the three long weary years which remained to her of his life. She was rewarded by finding herself, at his death in 1914, quite comfortably off, and for the first time able to afford little comforts that mean so much to a woman—an extra car or two, and more than just the one tiara. (Many a time during her hard life has she been reduced to a few bare evening gowns, scarcely enough to hold body and legs together.) She settled down very comfortably at Biarritz, where the simple seaside life appealed to her after the formal splendours of Ekaterinbog, and her colour, drained from her cheeks by Fédor's dimly lit sick-room, soon turned to a lovely peach bloom under the dazzling lights of the Casino.

My dear readers will guess what shattered that brief respite. War—which came with such appalling sudden-ness to us all. I myself shall never forget that terrible day, which was graven doubly on my heart by a small Bengers tragedy. A favourite sow of Addle's had just presented her boar with a fine litter of eight piglets. But some germ must have attacked the poor little things, for by the evening five of them had died. Next day my husband came to me with a look on his face which betokened bad news. 'What is it?' I asked in alarm. 'Is it the children——?' 'No, my dear,' he answered gravely. 'The rest of the litter has died and we are at war.'

But to return to Mipsie. Those who have appraised my sister's character through these pages will sense with-out any word of mine that her career was vivid in the extreme. Strange tales are told of her during those fearful years—how a German spy once lay under her bed, jotting down notes, for one whole night; how she was seen in Brussels on Armistice Day seated in a gun-carriage drawn entirely by Generals. It is said that one should only believe half that is told, so these rumours may be false. Though somebody once said of Mipsie that you can believe 150 per cent, double it, and then add the number you first thought of! It was some time before my sister found her real niche in the war, and though, like all of us, she threw herself into work from the start, her early efforts were somewhat unlucky. She began by working in the Censor Office, but left early in 1915 owing to a stupid misunderstanding on their part, so typical of official red tape.

There was a certain Parliamentary Under Secretary at that time—I will call him Lord X—who seemed indeed to have every qualification for success; youth, good looks, money, brains, He was already forecast for a ministerial post in Government circles. Mipsie had met him several times and formed the same high opinion of him. What was her disappointment therefore to have a letter pass through her hands at the Censor Office from Lord X to a young V.A.D. in France, containing an offer of marriage. The girl was a complete nobody, with, obviously, none of the qualities suited to the wife of a coming man, who needed some one of intelligence and social brilliance —such as, for instance, Mipsie's delightful daughter Millie, aged twenty-four, who was working then at the Admiralty. My sister could not bear to think that a great career, possibly a future Prime Minister, might be ruined by the wrong marriage, so she deleted the proposal, and cleverly contrived to censor the letters that followed, which demanded, naturally, why the girl had never replied to his first offer. Meanwhile, Mipsie arranged that Lord

X and Millie should see plenty of each other, and I am convinced—suffering from pique and loneliness as he was—that another week would have seen the young couple happily engaged, when unfortunately the V.A.D. was taken ill and invalided home. The whole facts of the censored letters somehow came out and were unluckily attributed to Mipsie, who was requested to resign from the Censor Office in consequence.

She left with a sick heart, reflecting, as many great men must have reflected in the past, when their noble plans for their country's welfare had gone astray, how hard is Britannia's shield, how cruelly sharp her spear.

GREAT DEEDS IN THE GREAT WAR

I WISH I could say that my own life during the great war had been thrilling and romantic, as Mipsie's was, but candour compels me to admit that mine was the part of a very humble (except in birth) cog. There were, of course, my knitting parties at Bengers, where, being of an inventive turn of mind, I enjoyed spurring my workers on to new creations, such as knitted pyjamas for hospital patients, knitted scarlet bands for staff hats, etc. I still think that almost every manufacturing shortage could have been bridged by voluntary knitwork, but the powers that be usually lack my vision, I find. I actually knitted one whole field-gun cover in waterproof wool myself, and got it sent out as a sample to Havre, where the English authorities saw fit to despise it, but the more imaginative French used it for years, I am told, in connexion with catching langoustes, so my labours were not in vain. Another invention of mine was dog-basket cookery, on the hay-box cooking theory, only employing the natural warmth of a dog's body to heat a specially-shaped dish, concealed beneath a cushion. It only failed because the dogs used in experiments *would* 'make their bed', discover the food and then eat it. Apart from these homely occupations I cannot boast of any excitements at Bengers, and it is not surprising that Mipsie, who took sanctuary with us after her shocking treatment from the Censor Office, soon felt a longing for a more vital and active life. She did splendid work going round to recruiting meetings with

Addle, where her winning ways brought many a volunteer to the colours, but my husband found one day that she was giving all the recruits the traditional shilling encased in little lockets, showing the actual king's head on one side and her own likeness on the other. Addle is perhaps on the conventional side, and he considered this slight infringement of regulations ill-advised, and told Mipsie so. After that her enthusiasm seemed to wane, and she appeared restless. I encouraged her to help our working parties by reading out to us, but I must confess that her choice of books was not always suitable for village people.

One day her pent-up feelings broke out, after a specially long afternoon's work. Throwing the copy of *Three Weeks* which she had been reading across the room, she suddenly exclaimed: 'Blanchie, I can't go on here any longer. I'm going to France, or anyway to London. I must get closer to our men.' Who shall blame her for following the dictates of her glowing heart?

There was at that time a great appeal for châteaux and hotels well behind the firing lines to be offered as convalescent homes to relieve the hospitals. Mipsie immediately offered the beautiful château of her friend, the Duc D'Aperitif, who was, of course, fighting, so she took his consent for granted, and was soon installed there, making all arrangements for staff and seventy beds for French officers. What was her surprise and dismay when a car drove up to the château one day, containing—the Duchesse D'Aperitif! The Duc in his friendship with my sister had never mentioned that he was married, so she can hardly be blamed for acting in ignorance of the fact, but unfortunately that did not help matters with his wife, who for some unknown reason seemed incensed at Mipsie running a convalescent home at the château, when she had (so she said!) returned with the express purpose of doing so herself. However, possession is nine-tenths of the law, so, after a very exhausting half-hour for my poor sister, the Duchesse left, threatening to open a home at the large, and before the war very fashionable, Hôtel D'Angleterre at Coquille Plage *one mile away*! The small-mindedness of some women is truly amazing. As Mipsie said, when all that mattered was the wounded soldiers, how any one could argue about such trivial things as property just passed belief, but the fact remains that the Duchesse did set up what amounted to a rival convalescent home, and what is worse, tried by every means in her power to make it a greater success than the Château D'Aperitif, where poor Mipsie had to labour under many disadvantages—out-of-date equipment, shortage of bathrooms and so on; whereas the Hôtel D'Angleterre was, of course, completely up-to-date in every way. My sister sent down almost daily complaints and demands for new domestic utensils. They were completely ignored. In self-defence Mipsie had then to ignore the Duchesse's orders requisitioning the garden produce from the château. This rivalry became known in the village as *la bataille de 'rouge et noir*,' because the Duchesse always appeared in smartest black, while Mipsie dressed very simply in pure white chiffon, her only colouring being a red cross embroidered in tiny garnets on her snowy head-handkerchief, and a bright scarlet arm-band bearing the letter B and the Briskett coronet in semi-precious stones. (For with wonderful loyalty to her first husband, she always returns, after each marriage, to the rank and title of an English Duchess.) The bitter struggle continued for four months, then suddenly, the Duc D'Aperitif appeared one day and confronted Mipsie in her office in the Duchesse's boudoir. He told her that she would have to go. That his wife insisted, and the law was, unfortunately, on her side. Mipsie's eyes blazed at this miscarriage of justice. 'If I go,' she told him, 'I take my patients with me.'

And that is exactly what happened. One week later my sister left the château with sixty-seven officers—unfortunately three were too ill to travel—and shook the dust of Coquille Plage off her feet for ever. It is not the first time that a worth while and noble work has been ruined by a woman's petty jealousy, no doubt, but it sickened my sister of war service to such an extent that she spent the following few weeks in sick leave, with her patients. Then the old, brave Mipsie returned to her real character and she threw her energies into the selfless struggle once again.

XX

HOW MIPSIE WON THE WAR
AND LOST THE PEACE

It was not until early in 1917 that Mipsie found her real métier in the great war, though she accomplished many wonderful things during the previous year, especially in liaison work, establishing a depot for Regimental Pets (though she was always the chief pet, as some admirer said), and as a voluntary inspector of Staff tennis courts. This last involved touring round the various H.Q's, often in great personal danger from her car skidding in ruts, and playing experimental games with the officers. Sometimes, of course, bad weather would preclude outdoor sports, so Mipsie would be the guest of Army Headquarters for a few days, and in that way she grew to know many of their needs; she often says that her Base memories would fill a book. It was these experiences that led her to open her famous Milli-Baba Café in Amiens. She realized that man's chief want in that grim and arid war was glamour—and she gave it to them with both hands.

Her first step, when she had found the right place— an enormous, almost empty wine cellar, which she and a few devoted helpers got completely clear in no time, was to appeal through the British Press for what she needed to give the desired atmosphere of an Eastern café. As always with Mipsie, the response was magnificent. She asked for beads—every jewel-box in the *beau monde* was opened to send her amber, lapis lazuli, cornelian,

jade. . . . She wanted palms—there was not a con-
servatory in the stately homes of England that did not
yield her of its best. Persian rugs, flowing draperies,
almost too many brass gongs (people were particularly
generous with Benares ware) poured into her depot at
our London home in Eaton Square, and were somehow
or other got out to France by my clever sister.

The opening of the Milli-Baba Café was almost as
brilliant as a peace-time function. The waitresses, who
were all dressed as houris, were drawn from the cream of
Debrett (for it is one of Mipsie's great boasts that she has
never been associated with the *demi-monde*—indeed, as
she has frequently remarked, half of anything is too little.)
So dukes and marquesses daughters handed round sandwiches which their mothers had cut up, and in some
cases their grandmothers washed the plates behind a
screen. Mipsie herself, dressed with war-time simplicity as the Queen of Sheba, dispensed champagne
from earthenware ewers. It was all very homely and
delightful.

Such was the popularity of the café, however, that she
was forced, after a fortnight, to close it for one whole
week-end, so that she and her staff could collect and
restring the beads which the waitresses had worn and
mend the rents in their *yashmaks*. It was then that they
discovered a Quartermaster fast asleep in a large Benares
pot which had been used as an ash-tray. He had been
there since the opening. This decided Mipsie to make
the Milli-Baba more exclusive, so that such incidents
should not be repeated. Consequently she was compelled
to raise her prices considerably, and this continued
throughout the war, the popularity and the tariff rising
above each other in a splendid spiral. There were some
maliciously-minded persons who hinted that Mipsie
was making 'a good thing' out of the venture and robbing

our fighting men.   I hope they may feel ashamed when they read the following facts.

We all remember the terrible time in the Spring of 1918 when the advancing Germans so nearly captured Amiens.   Then suddenly there came a check—a check which proved the first stepping-stone to our final victory. It was not till after the armistice that I was shown a letter, which somehow had come into British hands, written by a high-up officer in the German army to his wife.   In it he said that from all he heard about Amiens, it would be a bad thing for them if they captured it, as if the Duchess of Briskett was still there, Germany would have to *pay too dear for victory*.   Some say that the words were meant in joke, but in my opinion it is clear that, in fact, my dear sister was instrumental, if not actually responsible, for *winning the great war*.

But where others receive high honours, pensions and grants, Mipsie's sole reward was the consciousness of a job well done, and what small profits, amounting to a few thousand francs (or pounds, I forget which) she had made out of the Milli-Baba—money which was soon to save her from complete ruin, as my dear readers will hear.

One day Addle and I were quietly sitting at Bengers, he going over pig notes, I endeavouring to use up some tarred twine which I had had for knitted sou-westers (a little war wrinkle of my own) by crocheting a jumper for Margaret, then an adorable little ruby-faced imp of six, when Mipsie burst into the room, with tears the size of her pearls (almost) coursing down her cheeks.   'Blanche,' she said wildly, 'the Russian revolution has spread to Goulashia.   They have imported bombs that really go off.   The palace is destroyed, Mich has fled, and I——' She staggered to a chair.   'My money is worth nothing.' I thought she was going to faint, and told Addle, who was standing sympathetically by, keeping only one finger on a design for pig-feeders, to ring for brandy, but when it came she seemed to rally as she helped herself to a tumbler full. 'It's the shock,' she apologized with her winsome smile, as she drained it.

'Dearest Mipsie,' I told her, 'you will surmount this as you have surmounted other troubles. Meanwhile you will, of course, look on Bengers as your home.'

Somewhat to my surprise, for he is very moderate as regards alcohol, my husband also poured himself out a tumbler of brandy and quickly drank it. 'I have had a shock, too,' he explained, catching my questioning eye. I think that incident shows the amazing devotion Mipsie inspires in all, that Addle, who is by no means emotional, could thus feel her troubles as his own.

XXI

MILLICENT

I FEEL that I should really apologize to my dear readers for this chapter, because it is largely about myself, which is a sad come-down from the colourful details of my beautiful sister's life.

After the terrible news of the revolution in her late husband's country and her own bankruptcy in consequence, Mipsie had once more to face the grim phantom of starvation—or starvation only slightly removed by the £3,000 a year allowed her by Oxo. Accordingly, she was forced to tackle yet again the problem of earning her living. She decided to open a hat shop.

She had found a charming little house in the depths of Mayfair, with a shop on the ground floor. The only difficulty was the price, which was high. But here she was helped by her new son-in-law, Sir Basil Warpe, whose engagement to her only daughter Millie Mipsie had bitterly opposed at first (he had gained his fortune and title from coco-nut matting, which is indeed a terrible thought in connexion with a duke's daughter.) But when my sister had seen him and learnt how kind and generous he was—he agreed to finance the whole of her new venture—she realized instantly that he was one of Nature's Gentlemen, and that solid worth was better than blue blood. The happy pair were married in the Spring of 1919, and a month later Mipsie opened her new shop under her own name of 'Millicent'.

For a while I saw little of her. She was frantically

busy, working day and night, she told me, to make a
success. Then suddenly I got a wire from her: 'Must
go to the Grand Prix to see the fashions. Can you keep
an eye on the shop.' Thus began my own career in trade.

It wasn't until the following winter that I turned to
designing millinery myself. The reason was that the
stock was getting low, Mipsie having been away in Paris
more and more, seeking the right models. (She has
such a high standard.) One day I happened to bring
up to London for re-covering an old red silk lamp-shade,
and to leave it carelessly on the counter. To my surprise,
a customer (an old friend of mine, Lady de Rusk, who is
rather short-sighted) took it up quite naturally and tried
it on, saying: 'This is nice and light to wear. I hate
heavy hats. How do I look, Blanche?' In a flash I
had draped a veil over the top and a feather round the
rim. 'Connie', I told her, 'it's your hat.' She bought it!

That night I could hardly sleep for excitement and
making plans for the future. I have always had rather
original ideas, many of which I have passed on through
these pages, so it may be imagined with what joy I
entered, during the coming weeks, into the new and
thrilling sphere of a creative artist. Scraps of lace from
my piece drawer, peacock's feathers, fir-cones, old Shetland
shawls dyed and stretched over wire frames, worn bedroom
rugs, the best parts cut out and used in toques—all these
contributed to what I could truthfully call 'original
models'. Some, of course, were more successful than
others. Before I learnt that feathers must be baked before
use, I made one customer a lovely Ascot hat from one of
our White Wyandottes, which she brought back to me
in a condition which demanded, sad to say, its instant
destruction. Another hat, with a pretty design in fish-
bones sewn on to velvet ribbon with raffia, was returned
and I had to refund the cost price, because a cat had eaten

a large part of the crown. On the other hand I had my successes, my real triumph being when I was asked to design the millinery for a whole West End theatrical production—a play called *The Cranks*. How proud I felt at seeing Mipsie's name on the programme which they sent me—alas, I did not see the play. My work was keeping me away from home more than I really liked, and though Addle never complained, I sensed that he felt it, so made a point of getting back to Bengers directly the shop shut.

After that success came sudden disaster. A charming model I had made of tree bark, painted in gay scarlet enamel unfortunately melted in a hot room and stuck fast to its owner's hair, most of which she had to have cut off in consequence. She brought an action against 'Millicent' and was awarded damages. I insisted, against Mipsie's protests (she had to return to England for the case of course) in paying these myself, as it was my fault, and then urged her to go at once, as she had planned, to Cannes, where she said the sea air always gave her inspiration. It meant my remaining in London instead of going to Scotland with Addle, but that couldn't be helped.

Two days after she had departed an extraordinary thing happened. A little elderly man, with a parchment yellow face and the air of a lawyer, suddenly appeared in the shop one day and asked to buy the business. He was acting for an interested party, he said. I cabled to Mipsie who wired back asking £14,000—just double what she had paid for it, but after all there was now the goodwill, which amounted to quite a lot, for the notoriety of the case had filled the shop. I communicated the price to the agent, who accepted it instantly, without one quibble. 'Millicent' was sold!

Now comes the strange part. I was resting on my bed

(for truth to tell I had found the almost daily visits to town decidedly tiring) one day during the next week, thinking how brilliant Mipsie was to have made 100 per cent profit in so short a time, when I heard voices on the terrace. What was my astonishment, on looking from my window, to see Addle in close conversation with— my little parchment lawyer! When I got downstairs, my husband was alone in the library, doing his Press-cutting book and humming contentedly to himself. I told him what I had seen.

'Nonsense, my dear,' he answered to my amazement, 'you must have been dreaming. I've been here the whole afternoon. You're over-tired, that's what it is, but Scotland will soon put you right.'

Which it did. But I ask my dear readers, can any of you explain the reason for that extraordinary hallucination?

XXII

MELISANDE

BRIEF though it was, Mipsie's experience in trade as 'Millicent' served only to inspire her further. This time she decided that a dressmaking business would give more scope to her genius. 'What is a hat?' she said, whilst discussing the matter with me. 'A few flowers or feathers, worth twenty guineas at the most. But a lovely gown has no limit, either in imagination or price.'

Once again the right premises were her chief difficulty, for she had only the £14,000 she had made out of the sale of her hat shop, since when relations had been some-what strained between her and her son-in-law, Sir Basil Warpe (he had some absurd idea that she should have repaid him his original capital), so she felt it would be unwise, or worse still, useless, to approach him for more funds. However, money has never really worried my light-hearted sister. 'Where there's a bill there's a way,' she often says laughingly. The right place must be found and the money for it would somehow follow.

We were in deserted Chine House—the Briskett's London home—one day, going through some drawers of family lace which she thought might be useful, when a sudden idea occurred to her. 'Blanchie,' she said excitedly, 'why shouldn't I open my dress shop here? Just think of the models parading down the great stair-case—it would be wonderful!' 'It certainly would, darling,' I remember saying dubiously, 'but what would Oxo say?' Mipsie reflected, then dimpled. 'We wouldn't tell him,' she said. 'He is always in Scotland now and hardly ever comes south.' At that moment the door opened and a tall, rather handsome girl entered the room. 'Will you please tell me what you are doing here?' asked Mipsie coldly. 'I am the Duchess of Briskett.' To our astonishment the girl replied: '*So am I*'! It appears that Oxo, in a thoroughly deceitful manner, had married again without a word to his former wife.

Eventually Mipsie took a shop in Bond Street at a high rent, and also spent a large sum on its re-decoration. Next she set about designing the models, and she appeared at Bengers one day laden with bales of lovely material and demanding some one to drape! We tried to persuade Addle—for I was unfortunately too plump—to help the good cause, but even though we allowed him to read his favourite book on pig-keeping while Mipsie pinned chiffon and velvet on him for one whole evening, he did not really enter into the fun somehow. But the second footman, Mipsie discovered, had an excellent figure and was very obliging and patient, besides being so good looking that Mipsie said his face alone immediately gave her ideas.

Eventually all her models were ready and Maison Melisande opened, with instantaneous success. Mipsie was clever enough to realize that with all the first-class Paris firms as competitors she must offer other attractions to clients beyond mere clothes. So the staff included a fortune teller, a racing tipster, and a private detective whose services were at the disposal of customers with accounts of £1,000 a year or over who were anxious to gain information about their husbands or friends. Then there were what Mipsie called her 'Petites Vignettes'. With brilliant psychological insight she realized that every woman loved to see herself as a different type. So

MIPSIE WITH HER FIRST HUSBAND, 'OXO' BRISKETT

for a few guineas a royalty could contemplate herself in the mirror as a midinette, a governess could look at her image dressed as Madame Dubarry, a welfare worker could revel in the feeling that she was Cleopatra. It was astonishing how popular these little 'let's pretend' scenes were. But most successful of all were Maison Melisande's Dress Parades for Husbands, which were arranged as follows: A customer would perhaps like a dress she had seen on an ordinary day. If she could afford it, well and good, if not she would specify that it should be shown to her husband (at an increased price). This simple scheme pleased both parties. The wives got more clothes and the husbands enjoyed the parades, which were exclusively for men, so greatly that they did not grudge the money for their wife's gown. And gradually Mipsie extended the facilities to include a telephone for every customer, so that a busy man could continue to conduct business in delightful surroundings. But this very consideration for her clients led to more misfortune.

The switchboard for the various telephones was, of course, a complicated one. So Mipsie, who never considers herself too grand for any menial job, always insisted on taking over the operator's work during the Husband's Dress Parades, so as to be certain that efficient service was given. In this way it was inevitable that she should glean a good deal of City information, which she would have been scarcely human if she had not used to her own advantage. Unluckily, however, a big deal which she made in Ubango shares seemed to upset a certain financier, who was a regular customer of Maison Melisande's. He dared to accuse my sister of tapping what he considered should have been treated as a private line. The dispute became publicised, which led to the ground landlord of the shop—a strict Methodist—to pay a visit of inspection to the establishment. He could not have come on a more unfortunate day. He arrived towards the end of a Husbands' Parade and discovered a Cabinet Minister dancing the tango with one model, while a well-known sporting peer was telephoning to his book-maker, with another model holding the telephone on his knee. His impressions were worsened by several empty champagne bottles—used for local colour, Mipsie said—placed about the showroom. He gave my sister notice on the spot, and when she pointed out the enormous sum she had spent on re-decoration, he threatened a public inquiry into the conduct of the shop should she attempt to claim one penny. She was thrown out of Bond Street, a pauper—save for £3,000 a year and a small, pathetically small, fortune in Ubangos.

XXIII

AMERICA

ALL through history we read of good women who suddenly realize the hollow mockery of the world and yearn only to escape to some sequestered spot, away from it all. Some have entered convents; others have found solace in the simple countryside. Mipsie sought sanctuary in New York.

She was too sick at heart even to face the winding-up of Maison Melisande, so I undertook the business for her, though the whole thing was very strange to me. There were some items in the schedule of assets which I had *no idea* were needed in a dressmaker's establishment. However, it was all done at last, and Addle took me to Brighton for a week's change, which was very refreshing. Indeed, Mipsie's departure, which must have depressed him as much as it did all of us—for it is like the sun ceasing to shine when my radiant sister goes away—brought out all my husband's bravery and cheerfulness under adversity. The evening she sailed he seemed positively merry, and insisted on taking me to dine in a restaurant, then to a musical comedy and finally to supper at the Savoy—an evening packed with new experiences which I must admit I thoroughly enjoyed, though I felt decidedly fast, having supper with a man!

I was soon heartened by hearing from Mipsie that she was very happy and had already plunged into hard work —as always with her the sweet and womanly work of helping others—she was lending her face to encourage humanity by means of advertisement campaigns.

Her approach to the subject was, as usual, practical and businesslike in the extreme. She charged according to rank. So much to be photographed as a baronet's wife and earl's daughter—Lady Millicent Standing. A higher rate for her picture as the Duchess of Briskett, and more still as Princess Fédor Ubetskoi—for to her sorrow she found that the American public, though delightful, were sufficiently uncultured to place a foreign royalty above an English duchess.

Needless to say, that country of big business was not slow to take advantage of such opportunities, and during the following year—1924—Mipsie was in constant demand. Gallantly she threw aside all personal feelings, and with splendid impartiality she appeared both for flesh reducing pills and fattening tonics, and lent her support to every political party that was prepared to assess it at its real value. She featured in brilliant social functions wearing Fifth Avenue's finest diamonds, and at revivalist mass meetings, where she was once paid as much as $1,000 for one hallelujah. There were minor misfortunes of course, such as the time when she caught a bad chill advertising waterproof underwear at Niagra Falls (though she received substantial compensation when she threatened, in the interests of the public, to disclose the fallibility of the goods, as well as her fee for advertising them, so all ended well). There was also an amusing episode when she was engaged to speak to the Volstead Society in praise of prohibition and to an assembly of hotel proprietors advertising fifty ways of serving up whisky in disguise during the same evening. *She mixed the talks up* and showed the prohibitionists how spirits can be sent up in invalid cups, or sucked through a straw from an ice-cream soda glass with a false bottom, and so forth. But this proved one of her most successful demonstrations, as all the prohibitionists crowded round her and placed a record number of orders for her exhibits.

Eventually her work grew to such an extent that she was forced to combine several advertisements in one in order to conserve her strength. For example, she might be photographed in a bathing suit, contemplating a waffle with a dazzling smile. Thus, in one picture, she would be advertising the bathing gown in, say, a New York paper as Duchess of Briskett, a brand of maple syrup for a Chicago firm and forwarding a dentifrice campaign in California. It was a brilliantly daring idea, for of course each firm believed that they had exclusive rights of the picture. But faith can move mountains, we have all been brought up to believe, and as Mipsie said—if mountains, why not managing directors? Her theory was soon put to the test.

One day, early in 1925, she received a wire from the chairman of Block's Skin Bleaching Cream: 'Have just seen our picture of you employed by Kuddly Crisps Cereals. Please report to our New York office immediately.' Next morning, dressed in pearly grey which accentuated the whiteness of her face, with two tears shining like drops of glycerine on her cheeks, she entered the office of—her future husband!

'Mr. Block,' she said, 'no American citizen can possibly understand the agony of body and soul a British aristocrat suffers in work of this kind. If I am to preserve my health for the Stars and Stripes, you must——' but she got no further. In two steps Mr. Block was by her side, holding her hands in a warm grip.

'Lady,' he said (or it may have been 'baby'—Mipsie was never quite sure) 'I have been in the advertising world for twenty years—I am the author of seventeen books on the subject, including *Dandy Ads*, *Sex in Salesmanship* and *Psycho-Suckers*, and listen, Baby' (or possibly 'lady') 'I hand it to you that you're the greatest business woman I have ever met.   What will you take to come into partnership with me?'

Well, my dear readers know how it all ended.   That evening Mr. Block arrived to take Mipsie out to dinner pushing before him a life-sized silver coffin entirely filled with orchids.   (He was just like a schoolboy in his jokes.) 'The old Julius Block is dead,' he announced.   'Since I saw you a new man has been born.'   Later he confided to her his hopes and aspirations—to graduate from a millionaire to a multi-millionaire, to have his solid lapis swimming pool at his beloved little twenty-roomed cottage 'Gnomeshome' fitted with a gold diving-board, and so on.   As he told her in his simple way some of these boyish ideals, Mipsie suddenly realized that a miracle had happened.

She knew that she loved again.

XXIV

THE LAST TRAGEDY

MIPSIE was married to Julius Keatings Block in the summer of 1925, and took up residence with her fourth husband partly at his Fifth Avenue apartment and partly at his beautiful Long Island cottage, Gnomeshome. As I said in my last chapter Julius was, although the wrong side of fifty and weighing over seventeen stone, just one big Peter Pan. He gloried in fairies and all the whimsies of elf-land till his dying day. But he was also a hard-headed and brilliant business man with an American's true flair for advertisement, so his house, which he designed himself, was an interesting combination of his varied qualities. As its name suggests it was a real home for gnomes. Every doorway was flanked by two gnomes who opened the door directly a visitor stepped on a mechanical contrivance beneath the mat. In the garden a small army of gnomes fishing round the lake would draw up, on pressing a button in their little chests, a pot of Block's Skin Bleaching Cream. Delightful little embossed silver gnomes sat athwart the bathroom taps, the turning on of which made the gnomes open their mouths and discourse on the virtues of a white skin. There was even a metrognome on the piano, to beat time with his tiny hand, while the piano seat was an exquisite orange toadstool, carried out in velvet broché with the spots in mother-of-pearl.

Like every foreigner whose heart is in the right place, Julius cherished a deep admiration for England and especially for the British aristocracy. So on his marriage, as a compliment to Mipsie, he had coronets fitted on every gnome's head, the coats of arms of all her family, including her three previous husbands, hand-painted on satin panels round the dining-room, and installed a picturesque half-timbered bar, over which he presided himself, dressed in hunting-pink and dispensing cocktails in gold tankards.

There was something irresistibly cosy and soothing about the atmosphere of this unusual house, Mipsie said. A little vulgar by our standards perhaps, but it comforted her to think of the wealth of imagination—and dollars—which had contributed to the home of this gay, puck-like, yet completely well-bank-balanced man. Nevertheless, despite their happiness, troubles lay ahead.

It was about a year after their marriage that Mipsie began to realize that her husband had some reason to fear for his life. Small things—finding a bill for a bullet-proof summer-house, seeing him slip a miniature machine-gun into his golf-bag—told the tale. Once he was sent a poisoned gnome through the post. Then came the terrible day when she was motoring out of New York and, on a lonely stretch of road, her car was held up by three men. One gagged the chauffeur, another drugged her maid, and threw them both out into the roadway. Then the three men took possession of the car with my poor sister in it. She was kidnapped.

They seemed to have no hesitation in telling her the whole story. Apparently Julius Block, besides being Skin Bleaching King, also made a considerable fortune on the side through the sale of illicit liquor. This he had only done since his marriage to Mispie, so as to give her the little extra comforts a cultured woman needs, and he lived in terror of New York and Long Island society and his brother Elks, finding out his guilty secret. The intention of the gangsters was therefore to hold Mipsie as a prisoner, until ransomed by her husband, with the threat of exposure as an additional lever to the unfortunate Julius. Mipsie, with her acute brain, took in the situation in a flash. 'Leave it all to me,' she told her kidnappers.

My sister has been bitterly criticized for her behaviour at that time. It was said—when the whole story unluckily came out later—that she had collaborated with her captors by writing pleading letters to her husband daily, telling him of her miseries and begging him to send more, and still more money, which she then, by arrangement, halved with the gangsters. If they objected she refused to write another letter. But they did not object. They appreciated a business woman's acumen and were glad, before they released her, to claim only half of the £800,000 which was eventually wrung from her distracted husband. It is said that they even offered her a permanent partnership, so great was their admiration.

But I know the true story, as Mipsie told it to me. She was, she said, deeply shocked to discover that Julius drew money from illegal sources and she thought the only solution was 'to teach him a lesson.' Yet at the same time she hated the idea of his parting with so large a slice of his precious fortune, so cleverly contrived to keep half of it 'in the family.' Thus, her seeming disloyalty to her husband was in reality a splendid wifely devotion.

Alas, their happiness of reunion was short-lived. Soon came the great slump, and on top an unpredictable bit of ill fortune. The fashion for sun-bathing suddenly came in. The bottom dropped out of white skins—and of Block's Skin Bleaching Cream. For a time they tried desperately to stem the tide by paying Hollywood beauties to keep white, commissioning Press articles on the vulgarity of tanned skin, even contemplating taking some of America's Society leaders into safe custody for a time.

The last was Mipsie's idea. 'Let's put the snatch on a Vanderbilt,' she said. She picked up a lot of quaint *patois* in the States.

But it was all useless. One day news reached Julius that sun-tanned arms had been seen at the English Court. 'It is the end,' he groaned. He felt he could not face telling Mipsie the tragic news. They found him in his office later—shot through the head.

At his funeral thirty-six cars carried the flowers alone —many in the form of gigantic toadstools. There was a purple pall embroidered with a huge gnome in golden sequins. Yet even that, as a friend said, had its tragic side. In his hey-day the sequins would have been of solid gold.

XXV

DECORATIVE INTERLUDE

As she journeyed back to England, utterly alone on the *Aquitania*, Mipsie's sad thoughts had once more to turn to the question of her living—what to embark on and who was to finance it, for she was now decidedly past her first youth and it came hard to contemplate, after so many years in business, using her own capital. Still, as she so romantically put it: 'If real gilt-edged beauty is a woman's stock the market will never be dull.' And this dictum was soon proved.

She had, of course, instantly attracted attention and admiration on board ship, partly by reason of her looks and partly by her deep mourning, unrelieved by any jewels except a triple rope of pearls, a solitary solitaire ring, a few simple diamond bracelets and a large sobbing gnome in brilliants, the tears being executed in sapphires, which was her husband's last commission to his jewellers before taking his life. It was a touching memento of him which she was proud to wear and only sold when she reached England because she was, unfortunately, allergic to gnomes, especially on the person. But to return to the *Aquitania*.

A certain millionaire peer, who I will call Lord B, was also crossing to England, and was just the type of financier Mipsie was seeking. A chance remark of his, when she had made some comment on the decoration of the ballroom: 'But you are the chief decorator, Lady Millicent,' gave her an idea. She had always loved the home beautiful. Why not consecrate her talents to the décor profitable? Lord B seemed only too anxious to finance her. By the end of the voyage he had reached his goal and Mipsie knew that her future was assured.

She started 'Millicent Briskett' at a time when there was still the craze for modern furniture and decoration. With her usual thoroughness Mipsie threw herself into the trend, and indeed added several new ideas herself. Many will remember her drainpipe tables and her wire-netting sofas, which made a lasting impression on all who encountered them. 'Strip, strip and strip again—and then begin constructive work,' was her motto. She held that humanity, silted up by ennui, needed everything new to refresh its jaded palate. So she designed glass tables and wooden tumblers, tea-sets of metal and spoons and forks of china. It was all rather beyond my humble brain and Addle became quite angry when I let Mipsie redecorate his study as a surprise after a fishing holiday. He said he 'wouldn't have his house turned into a damned operating theatre.' So sadly I sent everything back and replaced the old stag's heads (Mipsie had installed chromium cats) and Morris wall-paper. One or two other clients did the same, I believe, and it was most unfortunate that Lord de Quinsy's little daughter fell down in a kind of fit on seeing the nursery which Mipsie had designed for her for the first time. The indisposition was only a coincidence, of course, but it created a bad impression.

Luckily, however, my sister's guardian angel never quite deserts her and at about this time her own taste underwent a drastic change and swung right over to the antique. She held that humanity, instinctively ruled by fear, clung to established forms. From then on she sought only the mellowed, the time-worn, the faded and the worm-eaten. She delighted especially in finding for her American clients what she well knew, from marriage to

Julius, they would most appreciate, 'a bit of olde England.' No trouble was too great for the discovery of these precious relics. She would send her scouts into every little inn and lonely farmhouse in the country, while she sat at the end of a telephone at Claridge's, scarcely daring to move, lest one of them should telephone with news of a new purchase. She was very clever too in converting unusual objects for domestic use. A gibbet for a lamp standard, an old mill-stone for a fender stool, bag-pipes for cushions and so forth.

From 1934–1938 her business was most successful and I was beginning to hope that her luck had turned and her disasters were all behind her. Alas, how wrong I was.

She dealt, naturally, in pictures as well as furniture, though she was always a little diffident about these, feeling a lack of the highest expertise. (Tiresome little things such as Van Eyck and Van Dyck having names so similar confused her.) Always over-conscientious, she would insist on going to see any picture purchased from her hung, so as to be certain it was well placed. Often she would take it back to re-frame.

Suddenly a client who had just returned from America startled her by saying that he had seen the Vermeer which he had bought from 'Millicent Briskett' in a private house in Washington. Its owner had purchased it from Mipsie too, and both clients had paid the price of an original Vermeer. Unfortunately the story got about, and in less than a month twelve other clients had had their pictures, which they bought as old masters, pronounced as fakes by experts. All had let the canvases be sent back to Mipsie for re-framing.

My sister was appalled. Could she conceivably have mixed the pictures up while they were at the shop? It was not an impossibility, for she was always adorably vague. She could only plead her ignorance and beg, with many tears, her clients' forgiveness. She visited each one in turn and all agreed not to prosecute—except one. He was a chartered accountant. 'No figure means anything to me except on paper,' he told Mipsie bluntly. He brought, in 1939, an action against her for fraud.

How my dear sister, with her delicate sensitiveness and frail finances, would ever have stood the case I know not. I was already considering selling my tiara, after having it copied (Mipsie knew all about having copies made to order—so clever of her) so that Addle need not know, when the last great calamity broke upon us all on that fatal September day. The chartered accountant, thank Heaven, agreed to drop the case and Mipsie was saved. We must all remember that Hitler did that one good thing in his life.

XXVI

LIFE GOES ON

THE outbreak of the European war found my sister, in spite of the terrible blows which Fate had dealt her, still gallantly carrying on—'faint yet persuing', 'bloody but unbowed.'

Her first act, in accord with her life-long patriotism, was to offer her little house in Mayfair to the Government at a ridiculously small rent (it was just crass stupidity that made them disregard the offer) and to take a delightful small manor house in Buckinghamshire instead. Here she did splendid work entertaining tired ministers and officers of high rank but low powers of resistance, for charming and refreshing week-ends. Her altruistic work was brought to a sudden end by the warning of no less than seven evacuees! Mipsie felt that the peaceful atmosphere so sorely needed by war workers would be shattered, so quickly sub-let the house. Luckily, her notorious bad memory stood her in good stead at this juncture; she completely forgot to mention the evacuees, so let the manor at a substantial profit, which came in very handy on her return to London, where she felt that to live at a first-class hotel was the only way to preserve her strength for her country.

One of her most constant week-end guests—Major-General Bull-Mastiffe, now procured her a job as his driver, and after a week's delay—while she was waiting for her own tailor to make her uniform—she took up her new work, and for six months carried on these useful

though onerous duties, until an unfortunate misunderstanding lost the War Office one of their most tireless and
skilled employees.   One evening the General asked Mipsie
to drive his Adjutant, Captain Quickly, to a training
camp in Lincolnshire called Skindale.   My sister, with
pardonable ignorance, never having heard of the place,
motored him to Skindles at Maidenhead instead, and not
till they arrived—the evening being very dark—did the
Captain find out her mistake.   Being landed there somewhat late it seemed only common sense to fortify themselves with dinner, but though they of course went on
to Lincolnshire the very next day, the General, unluckily,
became most irate with his Adjutant, and almost as angry
with poor Mipsie.   A coolness sprang up between them,
and though my sister did her utmost to bridge it by zealous
attention to duty—often cutting short her daily lunches
with Captain Quickly in order to be certain of being on
time for her boss, it was useless, and in 1940 she was
advised to resign.

Soon came the awful time when England, as Mipsie
has so often done during her chequered life, stood alone.
And after that—the blitz.

Mipsie was always quite fearless in that ordeal.   As she
said laughingly, she was herself an incendiary bomb at
heart, and as for the black-out—'to those who have passed
giddy youth and have learnt wisdom, darkness is often
a friend,' she once said.   She was indeed a child of nature.

She was soon plunged in war work again, for she could
never bear to be idle.   So in the autumn of 1940 she took
on the managership of a Mayfair Beauty Parlour, and
helped in the unselfish task of preserving the youth and
glamour of those who felt these feminine treasures slipping
from them in the stress of the war.   It was a fine job to
do, all the more so as it was, at first anyway, uphill work.
Other well-known rival establishments, staff troubles and

shortage of materials were the main worries. She was unable to obtain the right substance for mud packs and so took up a large bin of mud from our sewage farm— unluckily there were one or two tadpoles therein (quite harmless, but customers are so silly). She tried to replace unobtainable henna with Condy's fluid but forgot that it also stains skin, and she lost a rich client of long standing during the ensuing dispute. But the staff was her real headache. As the call-up accelerated it was well-nigh impossible to get skilled assistants, and cleaners were more scarce still. Then suddenly, all her troubles were solved by her own genius.

She was working late one evening, trying to solve her difficulties, so late that almost her only remaining cleaner was already busy, sweeping the pile carpet vigorously. Sub-consciously, as Mipsie noted the lean, energetic figure at work, she could not help comparing her with some of the clients who came to her for slimming treatment and reducing baths. 'How do you keep your figure, Mrs. Meat?' she inquired laughingly. 'Just 'ard work, M'Lady,' came the reply. 'I don't 'ave no time to get fat.'

Instantly the idea flashed through Mipsie's brain. Why not kill two birds with one stone—let her clients clean the *salon* and reduce fat in the process, saving her also the eternal hunt for staff? The scheme was soon put into action and became most popular. The twenty guinea course included the polishing room, where Mrs. Meat would bring all the articles that needed rubbing up each day, sweeping with a stiff brush and an electric sweeper (specially recommended for redundance of flesh round the waist) and finally scrubbing floors—an advanced stage at an advanced cost, for Mipsie found that unless they had to pay more for it the clients would refuse that part of the course altogether. Afterwards came the special facial tone-up, massage and manicure, to put right any damage the treatment had done, and then the client would leave the *salon* a slimmer and a healthier woman.   None returned for another course which proves its efficacy.

It was only a step from that to another brilliant scheme. In 1941 Mipsie opened a Cleaners' Agency in Kensington, where for a substantial fee customers could hire out the services of houseworkers.   The two businesses were kept entirely separate and were never connected with each other, so it was sheer ill luck that one cleaner should have been inadvertently sent to *clean her own house*.   Worse still, on the hall table were two bills; one from the Beauty *salon*, another from the Kensington Agency.   She was not very nice about the whole thing and nor were other friends of hers who were also Mipsie's patrons. My sister felt that she could not continue if she did not have her patron's confidence, so she immediately closed the Cleaners' Agency and resigned her managership of the Beauty *salon*.

Another sad chapter in her life was closed.

XXVII

THE REWARD OF MERIT

IT is with a full heart that I pen this last chapter of my beautiful sister's life story. For three things have happened to give me cause for great rejoicing and thankfulness. Mipsie was released from jail last week, her sentence having been considerably reduced on account of charming conduct, she has just announced that she is engaged to be married yet again, and I am once more a proud grandmother!

Perhaps I may be forgiven if I refer to my own excitement—which actually happened several weeks ago—first. Those who read my last series in these pages will remember my dear girl Margaret, who wedded Private—now Lieut., I am thankful to say—Paul White of the West Indian Regiment nearly a year ago. He has proved a good and devoted husband, his poor sight getting decidedly worse, which is a blessing in many directions, one of the ways being that he hopes to get demobilized quite soon, when they will all live at Little Bengers Farm and Paul will help Addle with his pigs, which he can see quite well with his strongest glasses. I shall thus have my dear girl and little grandson for daily companions.

John Hirsute McClutch White—Addle insisted on his being named after him—is doubly dear to me because he is already the living image, both in looks and character, of his great-aunt Mipsie. He refuses to take his bottle unless he has a bright jewel on a ribbon swinging to and fro in front of him, and Addle, who adores his new grandchild, sat last week for over an hour on Nannie's day off, while Margaret was going over some linen with me (they are staying at Bengers) holding his pearl tie-pin so that little Hirsie could suck the end. He dared not let go in case the child injured himself with the sharp point and the moment he took the pin away baby roared. How we laughed when we returned to the nursery! It might have been Mipsie in that cradle.

But to return to the real Mipsie. My dear readers will remember the terrible tragedy that overtook her last summer in consequence of her activities in The Alert, a Firewatchers' Dance Club which she started in 1943 in a blitzed Mayfair cellar. In all innocence, anxious only to do the best for her men-folk, like any true woman (none of this dreadful equality of sexes for her; her whole life, she has often said, has been based on the difference between them) she bought rashly perhaps, and too trust-ingly from unwise sources. What did a word like 'black market' mean to her, who has never looked on the black side of anything? So she suffered for her ignorance, as others have before her. To our horror we learnt suddenly that she had been arrested, and subsequently she was condemned to twelve months in the second division. What an insult, not even to put a British aristocrat in the first division!

All through that dreadful time I have been her most constant visitor, and indeed have compiled this biography with the aid of the notes which she prepared for me. She has been the old gay, gallant Mipsie in spite of it all, though she has felt the privations, especially the lack of cocktails, cigarettes and man-power, most terribly I know. Yet even within those bare walls romance can bloom, as my readers will hear.

One of her kindest and most regular visitors was the prison chaplain, who also lent her his rubber hot-water

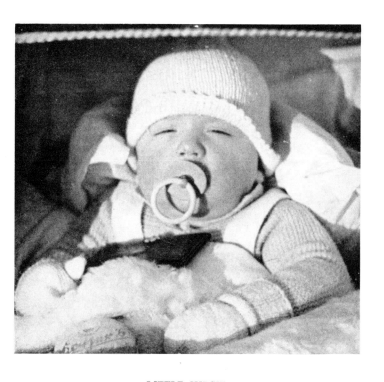

LITTLE HIRSIE

bottle—the act of a very *'parfait knight'* indeed.   He
talked much to Mipsie of her past life and made her
realize that she had, possibly, made mistakes which she
would fain undo.   Was it too late to turn over a new
leaf?   Mipsie, in the quiet of her cosy little cell, pon-
dered long over the words and the character of her new
friend.   She began to realize that perhaps the love of a
good man is better than titles and a homely hot-water
bottle more precious than rubies.   Then suddenly—in
the still watches of one night, a strange thing happened.
The worn rubber bottle split!   And as the warm water
flowed over my sister's feet and legs there flowed also over
her heart the conviction that she was no fit wife for a
clergyman.   Henceforth she was friendly to the chaplain
but not encouraging.

When the day came for her to leave she said good-bye
to many with regret—her wardress, who gave her a
parting present of all her clothing coupons, her fellow-
prisoners, many of whom were serving sentences for the
same mistakes that Mipsie had made, and above all the
Governor—Colonel Sir Augustus (Gusto) Royster, an
old soldier with a past record of gallantry and daring
and a present reputation of mellowed kindness and good
sportsmanship which made him popular with all.   As
Mipsie took his hand she found there were tears in her
eyes.   'I have never been so happy as under your care,'
she said.   'Please come up and see me some time.'   (I
don't know why she said 'come up,' for the sitting-rooms
of her little Mayfair house are on the ground floor.)

Well, my dear, dear readers can guess the rest.   The
Governor took her at her word next day.   He took her
out to dinner the following evening.   Mipsie learnt that
he was a widower, with a charming little place near New-
market and some good shooting in Scotland.   Within
a week they were engaged, and mean to be married as soon

as Gusto can resign from the governorship of the prison. Mipsie tried to dissuade him from this course, fearing that he would miss the interest of his work (as well as the salary), but he replied very gallantly that he would not need any more criminals to look after now that he had Mipsie. They will not be rich, I fear. But my dear sister, with touching humility, says that she has learnt much from her fellow-prisoners which will enable her, in spite of rations and shortages, to live with her new husband in a manner befitting the rank and beauty of, I feel confident that every reader will agree with me, one of the most remarkable women of our time.

LADY ADDLE AT HOME

THE AUTHORESS
An early photograph

TO

DILYS POWELL

AND

LEONARD RUSSELL

CONTENTS

ILLUSTRATIONS

I

INTRODUCTION

Bengers, Herts, 1944

MY DEAR, DEAR READERS,

In spite of the wonderful success of my first book, *Lady Addle Remembers*, which sold over 200 copies (this being a record for a peeress's autobiography, I am told, and considerably more than my old friends, Carrie, Countess W——, and Princess O. de la B. F. sold of *theirs*—but I will mention no names for fear of offending these dear people), I had determined never to take up my pen again. I felt I had put all of myself into that saga of my life, and that a heart bared once should not be bared again.

This resolve was strengthened by my publisher, whom I visited almost daily, and who showed to me, a woman— hard-headed business man though he might be—all the courtesy and sympathy I should expect only from my own family. 'We are glad you were satisfied with the book, Lady Addle,' he said, 'but the Directors do not feel they can undertake publication again.' I understood. They felt the responsibility weigh too heavily upon them. Indeed, the secrets of a noblewoman are no light burden.

But now, a new and clarion call comes. All of us have to play our part in this great struggle; to some it is to fight—indeed my own family are all 'in action'. My sons, Hector and James, both having done brilliantly in the Home Guard, the first being a Sergeant and the second a Lance-Corporal after only two years' service,

while my dear Margaret has a trusted position in the
A.T.S., being in sole charge of the gramophone at their
mess, and responsible for buying thousands of needles
in the year.

To others belongs the task of the Home—Dulce
Domum, as my father, who was a fine Latin scholar,
used to call it—to preserve the Domestic Front.

If my Front happens to be wider and more all-embracing than that of others, it is my privilege and my pride,
and above all my duty, not to hide it under a bushel, but
to show the Women of England what another English-
woman can do.

We have suffered at Bengers, of course. What home
has not? All the young maids and men have gone,
and we rely mostly on Crumpet, our dear old butler,
who is becoming so forgetful that he even brings the
port decanter in at tea-time! 'Don't stop him, poor
old chap,' Addle says. 'It might hurt his feelings.'
And he even drinks a glass each evening for Crumpet's
sake. That is my dear, generous-minded husband all
over.

It is the same consideration that prompts him to
walk up through two miles of park to the Addle Arms,
every other evening when I cook the dinner. (For
we have no regular cook now, only the North Lodge-
keeper's wife, who cannot come in every day.) 'It will
be one less for you to cook for,' Addle says. My heart
bleeds for him when I see him trudging off through rain
and even snow, but I am proud of his splendid unselfishness.

Then—back to my kitchen, for I have work to do!
Eight evacuees to cook for is no light matter. They have
offered to do for themselves many a time, dear good
souls that they are, but I will not have it. 'Hospitality
was the hall-mark of *my* generation if not of yours!' I

tell them gaily. 'Bengers is your home, and Bengers food your fare.' Besides, I like cooking. I would willingly cook for my three remaining servants (*noblesse oblige*) only they beg me not to. 'It would not be fitting, M'Lady,' Crumpet has often said, and I respect his fine sensitive feelings.

But indeed, there is nothing unsuitable in my giving cookery advice. For was not my old home, Coots Balder, noted for its cuisine? There is scarcely a crowned head that hasn't enjoyed our scrambled eggs, which were always served on toast cut quite simply in the pure shape of a coronet, or our famous black currant jelly (a jelly made from black currants), a tiny pot of which was packed in every visitor's trunk when they left. How well I remember my brother Humpo,[1] who was an incorrigible practical joker, substituting a jar of live black beetles in King Ferdinand of Roumania's luggage. We heard afterwards that H.M. was very angry because they got out somehow and crawled into his sponge! Foreigners, of course, have not our sense of humour.

But to return to cooking. My dear mother was determined, though born in the purple, that we should know something of the sterner side of life. So each day one of us would accompany her to the kitchen, to go through the day's menus and translate them into French. I can see them now, neatly written out by the cook, who would also place a strip of purest white kitchen paper in every page we should need in the dictionary. I think my love of kitchen work started from that time, and my love of inventing names of dishes too! For I would often vary the menu by substituting an English name, in compliment to one of our distinguished guests. Gladstone Puffs, Chamberlains on Horseback, Pickled Prince,

[1] The Hon. Humphrey Coot.

Délices de Pankhurst (this last came later, after I married, when I espoused the cause of my sex very wholeheartedly), were some favourites. Even to-day I stick to menus, and have tried to keep Bengers up to date with such dishes as Bevin Hotch Potch, All Clear Soup and Joad-in-a-Hole.

But more of these frivolities anon.

II

HAPPY CHRISTMAS

ALTHOUGH these notes are to be devoted mainly to
cookery I cannot resist telling you some of the things
I contrived for gifts last Christmas, as they may be
useful to you through the year for birthdays, or even
weddings.

All of us adore Christmas, but perhaps we Coots
regarded it with a very special feeling, and I never
remember a Christmastide at home when we did not
decorate the house with holly, hang up our stockings, and
give each other presents. Yet there was no ostentation
about these last, my father's annual present to us children
being simple in the extreme, almost austere: just one
large beautifully cut diamond, which was then sent to
our family jeweller to be added to the *parure* which was
only completed on our fifteenth birthday. Even so, my
mother feared we might become over-confident and
perhaps blasé with the gift. 'Never forget, children,'
she would say, 'that there are many little girls whose
mothers and fathers can only afford to give them sapphires,' and in this way she maintained in our childish
minds a fine sense of proportion.

But to return—or rather to jump forward—to last
Christmas. How difficult it was, what with coupons and
high prices and the shortage of everything! There were
books of course, though many of these, my own poor
work included, gave their lives for their country (2,764
out of the original edition of 3,000 having been blitzed
in the publisher's bindery), so as I did not know anything
I was *sure* my friends would like I had to think again.

Here goes, then, with a few suggestions for improvised gifts.

Flowers. This is a problem for all—what to put on the dinner-table, what to put in the drawing-room. We all love flowers, though I think I have never seen anyone with such a passionate love of orchids as had my sister Mipsie (who, after the sad failure of her fourth marriage, has gone back to her first name of Duchess of Brisket). She would come in any day, while in the heyday of her beauty, with great armfuls of the lovely blossoms— yet she always seemed to want more. 'You don't understand, Blanche. It isn't the flowers. It's what they represent,' she would say. Indeed, ardent flower-lover though I have always been, I have never reached quite that point of mysticism.

But even in war-time flower decoration can be managed with a little ingenuity, as the following will show:

Potato-Peel Poppies. This, I fear, robs the pigs somewhat, but I am sure the generous fellows would not grudge the peelings of six large potatoes, which is all you need for a vase of six splendid poppies to set your friend's room ablaze. Just peel your spud (rather a vulgar word this, but I am a country-bred lass, so must be forgiven it) in petals, not rings, paint them in gay scarlet enamel, and—when they are quite dry— wire them on to strong twigs for stems. A black button from your good man's old waistcoat will serve as a centre.

Soup-Tin and Tennis-Ball Water-Lilies. Yes, you will never believe it, but it is just as easy to guide your tin-opener in the shape of a flat water-lily leaf, which can either be painted, or left—a faery gleam of silver, floating in your rose bowl! For the flowers, cut old tennis-balls in half and shape them in cunning petals with a pair of sharp scissors, colour them yellow, white, pink, red—let yourself go!—and your friends will be struck speechless when they see the result.

Patriotic Match-boxes. What could be more dull and inartistic than a match-box lying about the house? But paint and stick a Union Jack on each side, cut out any figure of a soldier, sailor or airman from an illustrated paper, and stick him on cardboard, with a cardboard flap to stand him upright like a photograph frame; put a hat-pin through the match-box end and then through the man's arm so as to appear as if he were waving aloft the flag of his country, and you transform a commonplace article into an inspiration.

And while on the subject of match-boxes, delightful ash-trays can be made from squat potted-meat glasses, by coating the outside with glue and sticking on bacon rinds in graceful flowing designs. Then hey presto!— roll the whole thing in sand quickly. The result has a rich embossed look, if a somewhat unpleasant odour. And don't forget to eat the potted meat first!

I could go on for ever, giving you all hints for cheering your loved ones and beautifying their homes. Face-flannels made into bunnies, with press-studs for eyes and a safety-pin mouth; egg cosies fashioned from old socks, embroidered in raffia; smart hats made from old felt slippers, and cosy slippers constructed by cutting up and piecing together old felt hats.

Perhaps I am unusual, but I do like to make a point of giving a present which will please the recipient. That is why I was so touched when my friends and family thanked me so warmly. My evacuees (I accompanied each gift with a little cheque) literally beamed with pleasure.

As for my dear Mipsie, she wrote:

'DARLING BLANCHE,
      'I love my little match-box stand with the pearl-headed hat-pin. Surely that was the real pearl pin which Uncle Ally gave you? Thank you, darling, for making it so beautifully, you clever thing.
                        'Your ever loving,
                                'MIPSIE.
  'P.S.—Don't forget to let me know about the pin.'

Mipsie was specially fond of Uncle Ally,[1] and would treasure even a hat-pin (it was a real pearl, by the way) for his sake. Ah, but we had large hearts in the good old days.

[1] Allick, sixth Duke of Droitwich, my mother's brother.

My grandmother, the Duchess of Droitwich, died when I was still in my teens. We were staying with her at Great Goutings for Christmas when her sad death occurred, and the double event made a deep impression on my youthful mind. I was already seeking to emulate my dear mother, who was a real poetess, and whose beautiful verses I quote several times in these pages. The little poem given below shows, I hope, how eagerly my girlish footsteps were seeking to plant themselves in the sod which her dear feet had dinted.

A WHITE CHRISTMAS

Everything's white this Christmastide.
The snow lies white on the terrace wide,
And the gardeners frozen stiff outside
     Are white, white.

White is Grandmama's face, deep lined,
With her pure white Irish linen behind,
And her will, but yesterday evening signed,
     Is white, white.

White are the wreaths which Potts[1] is preparing,
For a hearse may soon her away be bearing,
And the angels that greet her will all be wearing
     White, white.

[1] The head gardener at Great Goutings.

III

CRÊME DE LA CRÊME

LAST week I wrote about soup tins. To-day I am going to tackle soups.

My father used to say that every dinner should commence with this refreshing and stimulating course. 'What, no soup?' he would cry indignantly, if it had by chance been omitted in favour of oysters or cavaire (hors-d'œuvres were considered rather Frenchified and *risqué* in those days). 'Where's the soup?' He had a singularly clear and direct mind, which enabled him, I have often noticed, to go straight to the root of any subject. The hall-mark of genius, I have heard it called.

And what soups they were! So clear that you could almost see the soup-plate through them—or so thick that the spoon would stand upright in the tureen if you held it. I remember when it was the fashion to scatter letters of the alphabet cut out of vegetables—thin as wafers they were—in the clear soups; and what fun we had with them. My brother Humpo used to be rather naughty and contrive special letters for special people. P I G he dropped in the plate of a famous gourmet, and I O U for a certain duke who shall be nameless, whose debts were the talk of society. He only meant it as a subtle joke, of course, but some people were stupid enough to take offence, and my father had to forbid the fun.

As for Mipsie, her romantic nature got the better of her, as always, and I never remember a dinner-party when she didn't contrive to fish L O V E out of her plate and lay it, with her bewitching roguish smile, in front of one of the young men seated next to her, who would of course blush scarlet with delight and remain dumb with happiness for the remainder of the meal.

But these are soups of the past, and it is the present we have to deal with. No game stock, no sherry, no cream, no dainty alphabets to enliven dinner. So what then?

My husband says I am nothing if not inventive—and indeed, I am proud to be so. Even at the age of five, when I had burnt the ringlets off a favourite doll (pretending to singe them), I recollect that I insisted on having the hair of one of the housemaids, which just matched Evelina's, cut off and stuck on the doll's head instead. In those days one's servants were proud to share in the life and happiness of their betters, even in trifles like this. But I digress.

Here are some of my own little inventions which may help you to make your soups delicious, even in war-time.

Stock. Game and chicken stock is wellnigh impossible. Beef and mutton stock often hard to come by. But is there not one species of game which the Government tells us to hunt, and hunt with a will? I refer to the rat.

Rat stock (young and tender rats are best) is made on just the same principles as all other stocks. But be careful to skin your rat first. I omitted to do this the first few times, and I must confess that the soup *did* taste rather hairy in consequence. Now I flatter myself that I have brought my 'Bisque d'Horreur,' as I playfully call it— for who has not a horror of the live rat?—to a fine art. (Even Addle, the only time he ate it, complimented me on the title.) My evacuees take it with plenty of Worcester sauce, but that of course is a matter of taste.

Sherry again is an impossibility to-day. But why be

so conservative with your flavouring? Ginger-wine,
lime-juice cordial, even a little coffee essence will make
your soup distinctive and unforgettable.

Cream is another rarity. Indeed I can scarcely write
the word without nostalgia. For did we not have our
famous herd of Balder goats, which yielded the most
wonderful milk in England? Snow-white they were,
except for dun faces and chests,brown legs and a broad
stripe of black down the back. I can never think of our
splendid park without seeing the graceful creatures grazing
on the emerald turf. One of them, indeed—an old nanny
called Pixie—was promoted to the gardens in her old age,
and allowed to roam at will, even in the sanctum sanc-
torum of my mother's favourite haunt, the moss-rose
garden. And that reminds me of a curious story, which
I have never been able to explain. Two or three years
after my beautiful mother's death, my younger son Heccy
ran screaming to my arms, saying that he had seen Grannie
'in the wose garden'. I tried to comfort him by pointing out that it was impossible, Grannie having been in
heaven for years, but he persisted with the story, declaring
that he had seen her clearly, dressed in grey and nibbling
a rose.

What did it mean? My mother adored all her grandchildren—she could have picked out any one of them in
a crowd without a moment's hesitation—but I always
think there was a special bond between her and Heccy,
which may account for the episode. Besides, who are
we to question the verity of a child's mind?

I have wandered far from soups. I know of no substitute for cream, but—let me give my readers a tip—an
ounce of starch will thicken and enrich a soup wonderfully. As for alphabets and such playfulnesses, here is
the recipe for my All Clear Soup, which I mentioned
earlier.

Mix a little beef essence with boiling water. Collect some really fine twigs or stalks from the garden and—having washed them well—cut them into letters or dainty flowerets, just touching the edges with gum to make them 'stay put'. Scatter into the soup and drink quickly before the gum melts.

IV

COOKS I HAVE KNOWN

SOME people have suggested that these cookery notes should include a few anecdotes of some of the famous cooks I have known. 'Darling Blanche,' writes my life-long friend Alice Pytchley (now 'The Dowager,' like every second person one meets nowadays), 'Your domestic front is delightful, but I can't bear to think of you working so hard. Why not write about real cooks, and give their recipes, which would help us all?'

Poor Alice—I have never met anyone, I think, who so strongly deprecates work of any kind. Before this war, she told me, she had never filled or emptied her own tooth-glass, or put the tooth-paste on the brush. She feels such privations very deeply both for herself and her friends, I know. But I digress.

I have of course known many famous cooks, from the chef of my brother-in-law, Prince Ubetzkoi (Mipsie's third husband), who could serve up twenty-three courses without repeating a single dish, to my brother Crainy's[1] Mrs. Mundle, who could make a simple six-course dinner seem like a feast.

But first in memory comes, as always, my old home, Coots Balder, and I immediately think of Mrs. Flack. What a martinet she was, and what a temper she had! As children we would sometimes hide in the backyard for the fun of seeing the saucepans, frying-pans, and kitchen-boys being flung, one after the other, through the window. When preparing dinner she would insist

[1] Viscount Crainiham.

134

on being entirely alone, except for the three kitchen-maids, who would have to be blindfolded when Mrs. Flack approached any part of the cooking which concerned her own special recipes. This led to an unlucky accident once, as one of the maids, attempting to move out of the way, blundered straight into the stove, where her cap fell off into one of Mrs. Flack's noted *consommés* just ready for serving. The latter, with pardonable irritation, but perhaps acting rather hastily, seized the great copper saucepan and immediately emptied the contents over the girl's head! But even that sad episode had its bright side. For Mrs. Flack, who had, in spite of her temper, a heart of gold, contrived specially for the poor girl so that she could eat it in hospital with her head and eyes bandaged, a cold *soufflé* of ptarmigan which later became one of our famous dishes. How true it is that every cloud has a silver lining!

Dear, generous, irascible Mrs. Flack! Even on her death-bed she threw an alarm clock at the niece who nursed her devotedly. And then she gave her the clock afterwards—a thoughtful and sensitive act one would hardly expect from her class. The curious thing is that the alarm never worked, I believe, after that day. Even inanimate objects, it seemed, loved Mrs. Flack.

I well remember the day when Mama told us, with some emotion, that Papa intended keeping a chef! My dear mother did not approve of foreigners, though with her loving disposition she readily forgave them this defect, realizing that it was their misfortune, rather than their fault that they were not born on the right side of the white cliffs of Dover. My grandmother, the Duchess of Droitwich, felt even more strongly on the subject of the chef. 'Bring a Frenchman into the house and it is the thin end of the wedge, Arabella,' I remember her saying. I shall also remember to my dying day, I think, my dear mother's answer. 'For better, for worse, was my promise, Mama,' she almost whispered, two tears, like vagrant Heavenly Twins, coursing down her glossy cheeks.

So Chef came. We hid in the laurels outside the back door, we children, and watched, with some excitement the servants' brake drive up. It stopped—and out of it sprang one of the handsomest men (my own family excepted) that I have ever seen. A flashing smile, a charming deferential manner and a graceful figure completed the picture. Chef was an instantaneous success with everyone. So delightful was his gay responsive nature that even the head housemaids seemed to go about their work with a lighter step and a brighter smile. As for his cooking, it was of course superb—though not accomplished without great extravagance and temperament. He would get through twenty quarts of cream, sixty to seventy dozen eggs, and two or three scullery-maids in a week with ease. But the result gave pleasure to all.

It was about this time, as far as I remember, that Mipsie became very keen on cookery. I'm not sure why, except that she was always adorably impulsive; also I think she was beginning to take life more seriously, as one does sometimes at sixteen. Anyway, nothing would content her but that she should have cooking lessons, and accordingly Chef was deputed to teach her. Of course with her brilliant intelligence and genius for throwing herself into every subject she takes up she proved the most apt pupil and the lessons soon became daily occurrences.

It led, however, to disaster. One day my mother, having some order for Chef, sent for him after tea. He was nowhere to be found, nor had anyone seen him for some time. A search was made and he was discovered in the kitchen gardens, showing Mipsie a cucumber frame. He was dismissed—after a painful scene with my father, I believe—for neglecting his kitchen duties and encroaching on the gardener's province.

I had intended to end this chapter with a description of one of the best cooks, in her own inimitable way, I have ever known—my elder sister Soppy,[1] who started the wonderful Back to Eden Health School. But how can one do justice to such a noble theme—she contends that, as Adam and Eve were the parents of the whole race, what they ate must be the perfect foundation of dietary—in a few lines?

I shall, then, make it the subject of my next what I like to call stove-side chat.

[1] Sophia, Viscountess Hogshead.

V

SOPPY

I HAVE realized since last week that it is wellnigh impossible for me to tell the world about my sister Soppy's wonderful school of Back to Eden Health Food Cookery without touching on her private life, which I omitted to do in my first book for fear of causing her pain. But now that—on the whole—all bitterness between her and her husband is over and she has made such a full and beautiful life for herself, I can perhaps dare to dwell, in only a gossamer way, upon the true facts.

Sophia married, in 1889, young Lord Hogshead—'Hog' as we called him—and for many years they were, with their little family of eleven, an ideally happy couple. Indeed people used to say that they, or at any rate she, were almost too devoted. If Hog was ever away from her for a day in London she would invariably send a footman after him to see that he came to no harm. It was the same with the children; I shall never forget how outraged she was when their eldest boy went to Eton and she was told that their Nannie couldn't go with him, if only for a week or two, to settle him in. Yet instead of making Hog love and appreciate her all the more for this wonderful wifely and motherly devotion, it seemed in some strange way to alienate him; and during the last war, when footmen were unobtainable and Soppy therefore employed a detective to watch over him at the White City (thinking doubtless of those terrible mountain railways), things came to a crisis. After a violent scene in which he dared to accuse her of 'spying on him' —of all wicked libels—Hog left the best and truest wife a man ever had and went to live in America.

For a time my poor sister was very unhappy, though her brave spirit never quailed, and she kept going by throwing herself into a hundred interests: Millinery for horses, Tanganyikan bagpipe music, soap-carving, a home for out-of-work shrimpers, and so forth.

Then at last she found her real *métier*—cookery. Yet more than cookery, for it has a fine and big ideal behind it; Back to Eden! Back to our first parents Adam and Eve, whose strength and glorious health were responsible for the whole race. What they ate must be the true foundation of all dietetics.

The basis of it is raw fruit (except of course apples, which are rigorously forbidden), uncooked grain, bitter herbs and milk—goat's or camel's milk if possible, though there is some difficulty in obtaining the latter just now. Soppy, who is something of a scholar, read an article in a digest describing how the primitive Eastern peoples used to make butter by putting milk into goat-skin bottles and rocking it to and fro. With her genius for improvisation she gives in her little Handbook of Health Hints an excellent way of achieving this to-day. 'Use up any old leather glove,' she suggests, 'by pouring milk into it, securing the top with string, and then tying it round your waist. The gentle movement of the hips will in time churn the milk into delicious—if rather strong—butter.'

I give two recipes which show a little of the freshness and originality of Soppy's theories.

Fig-Leaf Broth. Young fig leaves torn apart (no instruments must be used in cooking as there is no evidence of Adam and Eve having used any) and left to soak over-night in any little puddle which nature has formed near-by. The whole thing can then be scooped up and heated over a rude fire in a very rude pottery dish. Just before serving scatter some raw barley kernels therein.

Euphrates Salad (recommended for rheumatism). Finely shredded bulrush, laid out daintily on a bed of mixed river weeds. The whole moistened with a little bitter aloes.

It is very short-sighted of the B.B.C. to reject Soppy's repeated offers to give talks on the Kitchen Front—which boycott, coupled with the British public's perennial prejudice against any new idea, makes the Back to Eden movement somewhat slow, and it was, I know, a great disappointment to my sister when Mr. Anthony Eden refused to become president. Others, however, notably my own family, have given her every encouragement, dear Mipsie even suggesting if Soppy were, after the war, to open and finance a Home at Eden Roc that she would fly out every season and supervise it—asking only in return her fare and bare expenses at the Eden Roc Hotel.

Speaking of hotels, I must end with a strange story about Hog, who I forgot to say married an American girl shortly before this war. One day, in an hotel lounge, Soppy chanced to overhear two American women discussing Hog's new wife. 'What's she like?' asked one. 'My dear, lovely, but *quite dumb*,' returned the other.

Soppy was horrified. Music and beautiful sound had always meant much to her—she herself had one of the most lovely voices I have ever heard. To think that Hog had married a dumb girl shocked her deeply, and in spite of all she had suffered at his hands her generous heart warmed towards his poor speechless bride, and she sent her some of her Date Bark Balm, which has special properties for voice production. It evidently had the desired result, because Lady Hogshead wrote and told my sister exactly what she had said when sampling the gift; but I fear the whole episode proves all that we had already suspected—how low, how terribly low, Hog has fallen in his choice of a second wife.

TO HOG, ON HIS DESERTION OF
MY SISTER SOPPY

Never no more, Oh Hog.
Oh, what sad words.
Even the birds
Must weep,
Not cheep,
As they ever chept of yore.
The lambs
With their dams
Do repeat
As they bleat,
Never, never no more.

For your love is dead, Oh Hog.
You are, I think,
The missing link
In the chain
Of pain.
The crumb in the marriage bed.
The spanner that irks
Love's blithesome works,
The giltless gingerbread.

Yours is the blame, Oh Hog.
Naught will condone,
When alone
She sits
At the Ritz,
In discomfort and in shame,

While you go gay
In U.S.A.
Then Dog is your truer name.
Not Hog,
But Dog,
Oh Hog.

VI

A 'FISHY' CHAPTER

IT is perhaps specially apt that I should write something on the fascinating and many-sided (or should I say 'many-angled', in compliment to anglers all over the world?) subject of Fish. For at my old home, Coots Balder, were to be met with all the best and most fashionable fish of the day—I well remember how it was the custom for visitors to pick out the sturgeon they fancied for their own caviare from our famous Neptune Pool. (That pool is now a compost heap!) In addition to that my husband, Addle, is quite one of the most brilliant fishermen in England, and is the author of a very interesting book: 'Bites and Baits on the Bannock' (published at 25s. and now selling, with eight splendid full-length plates of outstanding fishes, for 1s. 6d.—a real bargain).

I recall many amusing stories about fish. A great friend of ours, Gugglie Gore-Blymigh,[1] who was one of the wittiest men I have ever met, was once being heckled during the hotly contested by-election of Ealing in 1908, and had just skilfully evaded a difficult issue.

Voice from the Back. Slippery as an eel, ain't yer?

Gugglie. That's why I'm standing for Ealing.

Of course roars of laughter greeted this brilliant sally, earning Gugglie many useful votes.

My mother's only unmarried sister, Lady Georgina Twynge (Aunty Gorge), was very energetic on the subject of cruelty to fish, who she maintained were quite wrongly

---

[1] Lord Gerald Gore-Blymigh.

called cold-blooded by callous sportsmen who didn't mind inflicting pain. She invented the Humane Hook for salmon, which doped the fish directly they took the bait, so that they couldn't be 'played'. This and other inventions earned her the name of 'The Fishes' Friend', but like so many reformers she got, of course, more ridicule than thanks for her work, one of her bitterest critics being, I fear, my own husband. I myself think it was a fine ideal, but perhaps a little extreme, especially for salmon and trout fishing, which is so much part of a Scottish holiday.

But I must stop these idle fishing stories—though they are not, I assure you, exaggerated—and get to business.

We of the old school have perhaps witnessed of recent years the greatest revolution in fish which it is possible to imagine, and one which it is difficult for a generation brought up on kippers at night clubs (which I am told was all 'the thing') to realize. 'Never,' said my old friend Emy Tottenham,[1] the other day, 'never shall a bloater pass my lips. I would starve first.' Yet Emy is now glad to obtain herrings, which she would never have tolerated in the old days. In truth, there is a new aristocracy in fish to-day, as in other things. My dear mother would have held up hands of horror had anything been admitted to the nursery except Dover sole, yet now our children are nurtured on plaice, and before the war I remember seeing my little grandchildren eating haddock and being apparently none the worse for it! It is, indeed, a strange world we live in.

For myself, in this as in other and deeper matters, such as education, politics, domestic servants, my motto is *noblesse oblige*. If it helps my country for me to eat skate, then I will eat skate. If I have driven one more

[1] Emerald, Countess of Tottenham.

MIPSIE AND ME AS ANGELS IN TABLEAUX VIVANTS
AT MARLBOROUGH HOUSE

nail in Hitler's coffin by breakfasting off kedgeree made
with dried eggs and frozen cod, then I am proud to feel
I am sharing in the rigours of war. But let us not
allow our standard to fall lower than is necessary. If
we must eat the fish of the bourgeoisie, we must, but
can it not at least be treated by Debrett?

Let me explain. It has become a necessity during the
war years, I know, to buy fish we would only have contemplated for our cats, or even for the servants' hall of
yore. Cod, hake, some upstart fish calling itself rock
salmon, another one called husk, with a far from pleasant
appearance. But the manner in which we cook them lies in
our hands. The French, I have often thought, are so clever
in the way they make the simplest fare appetizing, and
perhaps I have inherited something of this flair from an
ancestor in the eighteenth century who was, I believe,
half French. At any rate I delight to experiment with
such dishes as Dabs Dieppoise (with winkles and shrimps
in a little custard, which looks very much like the original
sauce, though it doesn't of course taste *quite* the same),
Grade A Salmon *meunière*, and Husk *bonne femme*.

The last was the cause of an amusing incident. *Sole
bonne femme* is, of course, cooked with a white wine
sauce and sliced mushrooms. I was anxious to try this
for I had been to a very interesting lecture at Harrods
on the subject of Fungi, at which I had taken copious
notes. All promised well. I gathered my fungi, sliced
and cooked them, made my sauce with a little ginger ale
I had by me and proudly served it up. My evacuees
pulled rather long faces, I thought, but of course they
were not used to French cooking and we English are
very insular about such things. But in the middle of
the night first I, then one by one, my guests, were
suddenly taken violently ill. Wondering what on earth
had happened, I staggered to my note-book and looked

at it again.   I then realized that I had stupidly neglected
to read the word 'not' in 'These must not be eaten.'
My poor evacuees took it all in good part—I told them
it was right to suffer in the cause of science!—but I was
very ashamed of my silly mistake, and insisted on treating
them all to a day in Watford, which they assured me would
put them right sooner than anything.

The colour of fish should be bright and clear. Remove the fishmonger's fingermarks with a little arsenic and polish with old lace.

Dab Skin, dried in the sun, makes a good non-skid covering for canaries' perches.

Some people get a red rash from eating lobster. But remember that many lobsters turn white after eating people. Mutual sympathy helps in every debility.

The best way to tell if whitebait are fresh is to look each fish between the eyes. If it squints, discard it.

If your goldfish are poor in physique, feed them on whale's roe, if obtainable. It improves the size of the breed beyond recognition.

VII

ENTRÉES

WHAT visions are conjured up—at any rate for me—by the very word 'entrée'! It is supposed, of course, to be the first meat course in a repast. But I always believe that the expression arose in my own family, in the eighteenth century, with the 5th Earl Coot, who was, I believe, a man of tremendous appetite. (It was the prerogative of the Nobility then to be heavy eaters. Nowadays every Tom, Dick and Harry aspires to the pleasures of the table.) Anyway, in spite of a ten-course dinner and a large supper, the Earl was, it seems, frequently unable to sleep throughout the night, and therefore a series of special dishes were prepared and brought to him personally by his devoted Chef, who would knock at the bedroom door, of course, to herald his coming. Lord Coot's joyous 'Entrez' would apparently ring through the house, and it is easy to imagine how the word, with slightly altered spelling, became all the rage in Society and subsequently passed into the English language.

To-day the entrée has more than ever come into its own by reason of its close alliance to the Salvage campaign. For with a little bit of meat here, a handful of left-over rice there, some flabby biscuits, half a beet-root—what a culinary masterpiece can be concocted by the clever cook! And one that not only pleases the artistic soul, but helps the British Empire as well.

The mention of beetroots reminds me at once of my dear Margaret, who is at present serving her King in the A.T.S. near Colchester. She has a somewhat florid complexion, and is also prone to blushing, especially over the cheeks, ears, forehead, chin and neck. Not long ago, while walking down Colchester High Street, a cheeky American private soldier called out in a quaint mixture of English and his native patois—'Hiya Beetroot!' which was, of course, the remark of a savage. But I am glad to say my dear girl showed both her natural wit and good humour under the attack. Quick as a flash came her answer: 'I'm not a beetroot'—and the discomfited American passed on.

Poor Margaret; it is harder, surely, for anyone brought up with an oyster in their mouth, so to speak, to be stationed in such a locality, than for those whose highest ambition would have been an oyster shell in their rockery. But she takes it all with the pluck of a McClutch.

But to return to the entrées. Half the battle, as I indicated before, is that the dish should look delightful. And in this we are particularly blessed in possessing very beautiful entrée dishes, all engraved with our initial and coronet, which gladden the eye and heart before you lift the cover and inspect the contents. Even so, this did not prevent a little tragedy which happened not long ago to what I am convinced would have been one of my most successful dishes.

I had left over from the previous day the following ingredients: A few cooked haricots, some brawn trimmings, a fair amount of porridge and some cold scrambled egg. (This last was an experiment of two days before, when I had tried mixing dried eggs with a little Hematogen instead of powdered milk so as to buck it all up, but it had been a thought too strong in flavour.) Well, I thought, here must be the makings of a good entrée if I can only set my wits to work. So I chopped up the brawn trimmings and worked them into the scrambled eggs—which had set rather hard by now—then arranged them on a bed of porridge with grated haricot bean scattered over the whole. Finally, I stuck in bits of left-over toast, so as to make a pretty rococo effect. The result looked, I thought, most professional, and I was delighted. But alas, for my pride! I left the entrée, in one of our most handsome silver dishes, on a side table, while I was called to the telephone. I returned to find that Gary Briggs, one of our little evacuees, had put the whole dish outside the back door by one of the dog's kennels, thinking it was his dinner. When remonstrated with by his mother —for it was after all in a silver dish—he said that he thought 'everyone eat off silver at Bengers', which delightful remark, of course, quite won my heart, and Gary got a hug instead of a scolding from his hostess!

To make matters worse, the dog—a favourite setter of my husband's—was very sick afterwards (of course, the dish was probably a little rich for a canine digestion) and Addle blamed me for the whole episode!

Curry, I find, is a very useful flavouring in entrées if one is not quite sure about the dish. Cheese also covers a multitude of sins. Sometimes, if I am *very* doubtful about things I have found that to use curry *and* cheese, plus a little nutmeg makes it almost impossible to find out what is underneath the sauce.

Lastly, I must tell you about what I mentioned in my first chapter: Joad-in-the-Hole. This is nothing more nor less than sausage meat (as sausages are not easy to buy nowadays) fried in batter mixture.

And I call it by that name because this war-time sausage meat, with only a modicum of pork in it, and ersatz batter, without one single egg, were never heard or thought of before the war, any more than was Professor Joad. Ah, but these innovations are hard to accustom ourselves to, for those of the old school like myself.

VIII

S O S—OR SAVE ORL SALVAGE

LAST week I wrote of entrées—those tempting little dishes which can so often be constructed from 'left-overs'. This week therefore I must say a few words about the mother of all war-time entrées—the Salvage Campaign.

It behoves both high and low to contribute to Salvage. And the Nobility have not shirked their share, however unpleasant it may be. I have one friend, who it would be indiscreet to mention by name, for Royal Blood flows through her veins, who faints regularly every time she lifts a dustbin lid. But does this deter her? On the contrary, she has had all her little personal pots, for face cream, powder, bath essence and so forth, specially modelled, at considerable expense, in silver, in the shape of dustbins, so as to accustom her to her ordeal. Her maid told mine that she now frequently faints when powdering her nose.

Another friend, the Duchess of Strewth (mother of Gugglie Gore-Blymigh, whom I have mentioned earlier) who was entirely engrossed, before the war, in social work among lift girls, has now switched all her energies to the rescue of bones instead, and has so far a salvation list of well over 1,000—a considerably better result than she achieved with her former work.

Perhaps the noblest job of all though—because it has been the most thankless—has fallen to the lot of a cousin of my husband's, Henrietta McClutch (Cousin Hen-Pen as my children affectionately call her), whose whole life was smashed soon after the war started, poor dear, by the loss of her brother's pack of hounds, who were dispersed for the duration. But she found, as others have found before her, that hard work was the only anodyne for sorrow, and she did a magnificent job in her county by going round with the hound van and collecting nearly two and a half tons of dog's hair. When she had reached the second ton, and had sewn up every hair herself in pretty half-hundredweight chintz sacks, the Ministry of Supply told her that they had never appealed for dog's hair, and had no use for it. It was a crushing blow. She had to unpick every stitch and send just the sacks, which the Ministry said they wanted. It is just the kind of Government muddle which one expects, but which is so disheartening to people who are endeavouring to help their country.

As for our village, we have, through our Save and Serve League, of which I am proud to be president, not only done our duty, but thoroughly enjoyed ourselves doing it. We have organized rubber hunts in the woods, hair-pin drives in the village streets, hip and haw picnics and sloe outings. We have also adopted a poor unwanted pig, whose mother had died and whose father was unknown.

Then, our last Salvage Week I organized a mile of buttons, and sat at the receipt of custom myself, having first sent out a circular letter urging people to sacrifice one bone button off every coat and waistcoat of their husbands. I pointed out that a man will not starve or die of cold if he is short of one button, and I led the way by collecting from Addle's wardrobe thirty-one beautiful buttons with which I started my mile. But I must confess that the villagers were not very forthcoming with their contributions. They said their husbands made a fuss—so like men! I daresay Addle will be annoyed when he finds out, but the Salvage drive only took place last September and he has hardly had time to notice the deficiency as yet. He is, I have thought once or twice lately, getting a trifle unobservant with middle age. He even forgot his eightieth birthday last year!

But paper is the Salvage need which I feel most acutely. Indeed, I think the word 'paper' will be found graven on my heart when I die as 'Calais' was on poor Mary's. (A distant cousin of my mother's family.) I frequently write long letters to my friends calling for replies, so to add the answering epistles to my paper sack. I am also trying very hard to make my dear Mipsie part with some of the trunk loads of letters which she has had during her life, letters from the highest in the land, expressing their admiration and devotion to my beautiful sister. But so far I have had no success. 'My love letters are my capital, Blanche,' she says, smiling her roguish smile. 'There is many a letter in that trunk that is better than a five-pound note. You never know when a poor man will come into a fortune and you can never be sure when an old letter will produce a dividend.' Dear Mipsie. Friendship has always meant much to her, and it is like her to think of her letters as so many treasures.

But to return to Salvage. We had a most thrilling talk at the Bengers Hall not long ago, from a Government Speaker, who told us several very interesting facts. For instance, I think it was sixty tons of paper, that would, when pulped, make one anti-tank gun. Or am I thinking of bones? He also said that if everyone were to preserve *just the newspaper they read each day, and send it to Salvage*, it would, in some wonderful way, save the shipping space needed for importing glue for aeroplane wings. And if everyone were to produce just *one* old umbrella frame, it would mean so many tons—I forget the exact figure—of non-ferrulous metal for land-mines each year. These may seem like dry statistics, but they must be taken seriously for they are the life blood of our country.

IX

MEET YOUR MEAT

THE subject of meat is one on which any woman, surely, and especially a noblewoman, must shrink to write? My grandmother, the Duchess of Droitwich, who was one of the most fastidious people I have ever known, always used, when driving in an open carriage, to start out equipped with a little mask (made of black moiré, I remember) which was freshly scented with rosemary each day, in case she should pass any butcher's shop, with its accompanying unpleasantness to eye and nostril. Then—up would go the mask till the danger was safely past! She was indeed 'one of the old regimé,' and might even, I daresay, be called a little eccentric nowadays. She also had, I recollect, a very strong aversion to governesses, and always said she could tell the minute there was one in the room. Another thing— she thought any mention of feet or legs indelicate, and such words as 'shoes' and 'stockings' were rigorously tabooed. She wore skirts sweeping the ground all her life, and every table or chair which showed the offending limbs was always draped in exquisite little shawls of berlin wool, made by grandmamma herself. She was very angry with my Grandfather, I believe, because he would never consent to do the same with his horses.

But to return to meat. Unfeminine though it may be as a theme, I am, perhaps, in a position of some little authority on the subject owing to my sister Mipsie who, it will be remembered, married as her first husband the Duke of Brisket.

Oxo, as he was always called, was at that time immensely rich, being part owner of the great Smithfield meat market, which had been completely rebuilt in 1868 with every modern convenience. He took his duties as a landlord very seriously, and it was seldom that a year passed without his visiting his property at least once. One day, when the late King of Portugal was staying in England, he expressed a wish to see the famous market, and accordingly Oxo made up a little party, consisting of Mipsie and myself, two or three other well-known Society beauties, together with their own or other husbands.

It was a glorious summer's day, and we all felt rather excited as we drove up to the great place, which was festooned with flags in our honour, while little frills of the Portuguese Royal colours were tied round every joint in the market. All the ladies wore blue overalls, so as to feel like real meat porters—I remember that Mipsie had had hers specially designed by Paquin—and there were as many footmen in attendance carrying fur coats in preparation for the tour of the great cold storage, which runs under the market for many miles. One of the Directors conducted us round and explained the whole thing to us very clearly. The King was delighted with the tour, and asked a lot of most intelligent questions. He was shown a leg of mutton and studied it with great interest. 'Our sheep have legs almost exactly like that,' he said after a moment, a remark which not only showed his expert knowledge, but seemed to bring our two countries very near. When we left the ladies were presented with charming gold brooches in the form of cutlets, the meat part being carried out most effectively in rubies, and the fat in topaz.

So I have always felt, since that day, if not exactly an interest, at least some little measure of specialized know-

ledge on the subject of meat. I sometimes even go to the
butcher's myself (my grandmother must be turning in
her vault!) and attempt to utilize that knowledge. But
indeed, in these present sad days, all the old landmarks,
such as sirloins, saddles, briskets, etc., are absent, and
one is sent away with some strangely shaped piece of
meat which would never have been seen further east
than Islington when I was young.

Nevertheless, as I have said before, it behoves us all
to cook our fare in a manner more noble than its appearance *au naturel*. I myself am a strong believer in the
theory that old methods are best, and that meat has
never been so satisfactorily cooked as on the old-
fashioned spit. Of course nothing like that remains at
Bengers, where the most up-to-date stoves were installed
in 1912. But we still have an open fire in the great hall,
and not long ago, with the aid of an iron hook and a clever
little contrivance of my own for turning the meat, croch-
eted in gay wools, I fixed up a spit and tried a joint one
day at tea-time. I thought Addle might object, but
beyond remarking that the dog seemed restless (he is
getting a little short-sighted, I fancy) he never noticed
the turning meat at all, until—hey presto!—my crochet
contraption suddenly became charred by the heat, and
the whole joint—half a week's ration—crashed into the
flames!

Well, I suffered acutely from that experiment, for I
was forced to buy liver for my hungry evacuees, and the
cooking of it is—or was—a real penance to me. I tried
handling it in old kid gloves, having several pairs to the
shoulder which I think it unlikely I shall often use again.
But the liver only stuck to the kid. Now I have a better
way, and will pass it on to those of my readers who are,
like me, revolted by the substance of liver. I have a
quantity of butter muslin which was used in the dairy

before the war, and I find that if I wrap each slice of liver in this it is far less objectionable to touch. Then, when cooked, I remove the muslin—or as much of it as will come away, that is. Indeed, in this, as in other things, I so often feel that Aristocracy is the mother of Invention.

X

GAME WORTH THE CANDLE

WITH what relief I turn this week from meat to game—from the foetid atmosphere of the butcher's shop to the heather-scented grouse moor, or our own delightful covers—the thickest and most luxuriant in England, I believe. (The brambles are so long one can sit on them easily.) Nevertheless, if the last chapter helped one poor housewife to baste her joint with a stouter heart, I am rewarded.

My own family have always loved sport. My father was a crack shot, and I have often seen him take a right and left at a runner and get it with the second barrel. My brother Crainy, if he had ever learnt to fire two or three minutes earlier each time, would have been more brilliant still. Even Mipsie shot occasionally, though she really preferred sitting beside one of the guns, especially in Scotland, when the lonely butts appealed to her love of nature.

Butts! The very word brings a pang, for my dear Margaret had her big—perhaps I should say her only—romance in one of these sequestered spots, when Billy Bynde-Wede[1] was staying with us in Scotland just before this war. I knew Love had dawned for my daughter, because she flushed up so whenever he approached her. And I felt sure it must be the same with him, although he spent all his time talking to a silly niece of Addle's—Di McClutch—with only surface prettiness, whereas for Margaret's beauty you have to look extremely deep. But I know how often this behaviour is a blind with the

[1] Second son of Lord Groundelder.

158

young, so I contrived, one morning, when the guns were being directed by my husband, to push Margaret into the butt with Billy at the last moment, at the same time pulling back Di on the plea of asking her after her parents. When we had passed I looked back. Billy was happily gazing at the horizon. Evidently he did not object to the change. My dear Margaret was blushing prettily with excitement.

What happened then I only learnt later. It seems that after a long silence Billy suddenly said: 'I say, I meant to ask you yesterday, will you marry me?' Overcome by these passionate words Margaret felt herself going crimson with joy, and she shut her eyes, trying to recover her composure before answering. When she opened them—Billy had gone! Evidently he took her hesitation for a refusal, for in a fit of pique he got engaged to Di that same evening. It was a sad end to the day, especially as it produced a record bag, I remember, of 960 brace of grouse and 427 blackgame—but not, alas, a husband for Margaret.

My love of sport has led me far from Domestic Fronts. But game is unfortunately no longer our daily fare (though Mipsie tells me she gets plenty—but of course she is a brilliant housekeeper) so hints on cooking it seem out of place. But rabbits are still occasionally obtainable, so I will tackle them.

The best way to skin a rabbit is to get your gardener to do so. If you have none, ask one of the tradespeople, who I find are always obliging and kind. But how to cook them when skinned? (The rabbits, I mean.) They are rather tactless creatures and don't go very far with feeding a large number. I will tell you how I got round this the other day.

First, I jointed my rabbit and rolled each piece in powdered ginger. Then wrapped them in strips of

tripe and baked them. It was a highly successful dish
both from the culinary and the economical angle. , For
my evacuees ate every scrap of tripe, leaving only the
rabbit, which I minced and served up later in the week
as savoury mock chicken croquettes. What was left of
these (quite a lot, it happened, because my evacuees had
had baked beans for tea, they told me, so weren't hungry)
I put as a stuffing in a ginger sponge which I bought in a
packet. Again, every bit of the sponge was eaten, and
I was delighted to have the rabbit for my all too meatless
pig bucket.

The mention of pigs recalls a story of a very narrow
escape I once had.

In 1905 we went to stay with the Archduke and Arch-
duchess of Lotharia for the wild pig hunting, which was
supposed to be wonderful sport. Archduke Blotto was
then about seventy, and considered by half Europe to
be mad—a shocking calumny on the kindest of men, who
had only one harmless foible—that he always imagined
himself to be some animal or bird. Sometimes, at dinner,
he thought he was a dog, and a bone was served to him
in an exquisite gold dish, on a beautiful Persian rug in
front of the fire. Sometimes it was a less convenient
animal, such as a giraffe, necessitating a long step-
ladder with a basket of straw at the top. Out hunting
he was usually a bird, and would just sit in the saddle
and twitter. One day, however, after we had been
there about a week, his fancy took a more dangerous
turn.

I had somehow outstripped the others, I remember, and
was waiting for them to come up with me, revelling in the
clear warm day, and admiring the traditional hunting
costumes of primrose velvet, when suddenly I heard an
extraordinary sound behind me, and looking round I saw
to my horror the Archduke approaching, snorting and

MY SISTER SOPPY WITH A WELL-LOVED FRIEND

snuffling like a wild pig. I realized with an icy thrill that *he was heading straight for me.*

It was an awful moment. If it hadn't been for the five attendants who never left him night or day, and who now closed in on him and drew his horse away from mine, I shudder to think what might have happened. A few moments later all danger was past. Archduke Blotto once more thought he was a bird, and—as though to recompense me for my fright—trotted up and with a touching gesture dropped a worm into my lap.

To Make a Peahen Pie.   Take a good dish, the size of two coronets, line it well with some thin slivers of fine ham, which have been five days marinaded in Canary.   Cast in it an armful of plumpe peahens, strewing on them basil, parsley, thyme, tansy and elderberry.   Now must you set about them peaches piqué with cloves and modest onions first boiled in cream, and lay on all a great quantity of the flesh of wild boar fine shredded.   Thereto 3 pints of good Burgundy, a glass of brandy, also a little water if the taste be liked.   When all has boiled for full fifty minutes the peaches must be removed.   After your dish hath reposed some six or seven hours in a gentle simmer, take from it the onions.   Now haste the boiling fiercely for a short space, and drain away all the fine brandy and Burgundy and the shredded boar's flesh too, to the end that these may make a noble manure when buried beneath shallots.   At length is your dish ripe to be set in the oven, where it may lie two hours more that the peahens be fully done and delicate.   Choose you the best parts of the breast only to serve upon toasted bread spread with foie gras as a light refection.

XI

A PLEASAUNCE OF PIG-STIES

Last week I wrote of wild pigs, and perhaps harrowed my dear readers by telling them of my terribly narrow escape from what would without doubt have been worse than death. So let me soothe them to-day by writing something of the delightful natures and charm of tame pigs—'Nature's gentlemen' as my husband so truly calls them.

Indeed, Addle is himself a considerable pig expert, having for many years personally reared our own special breed, the Bedsocks White. 'Treat pigs and butlers well and they will never let you down,' he has often said, and I must say, except for one butler who drank his Napoleon brandy and one pig who ate his wrist watch, it has proved completely true. Addle frequently supervises the mixing of the pig food himself, so as to be certain it is rightly managed. He won't even trust me to put aside the remains of some of my tastiest dishes, unless he knows just what are the ingredients. 'That's all right for your evacuees but not for my pigs,' he sometimes says, and actually makes me remove something from the pig bucket and put it in the chicken bin instead. He is not interested in poultry.

People are of course very stupid over pigs and think that anything will do for the swill, just as they imagine that pigs like wallowing in dirt, which is far from the case. I am sure our Bedsocks Whites are so clean that you could eat off them. Touching the first misconception, I am reminded of an amusing episode—though I suppose one should not laugh at it, as it certainly had its serious side.

Some old friends of ours, Lord and Lady Err and Stray (we knew them when they were Bob and Tootie Trespass), had at last, after eleven daughters, produced an heir, to Bob's great delight, and Tootie's infinite relief and thankfulness. The boy was of course to wear the famous Trespass Christening shawl, reserved for the Err and Stray heirs, with the somewhat superstitious couplet attached:

> The heir who wears not the Trespass shawl
> Will wear his manhood not at all.

So it is readily understood how the family treasure was valued. Well, the day of the Christening arrived, and when the baby was dressed, the nurse went to fetch the shawl where it had been laid out by the nursery maid a minute or two previously. *It was gone!* The most thorough search was made in vain, and the child had to be baptized in some other shawl. In spite of instant dismissal the nursery maid stuck to her story, and the mystery remained unsolved until—two mornings later, when a passing farm hand observed a piece of silk embroidery sticking out of one of the pigs' mouths. He pulled, and after a short tussle, for the animal seemed to have taken a fancy to the material (it had a design of acorns, which may account for this), the farm hand won, and returned to the house triumphantly with—the Trespass shawl.

The story was pieced together, bit by bit. A puppy had stolen the shawl, chewed it for a little and then buried it in the garden, where it was dug up by a stupid garden boy and sent into the house with the vegetables for dinner. Covered with a white sauce, it was served up in the dining-room that night but scarcely tasted, as the family were all too upset by the loss of the heirloom to eat much. The remains of the dish was then thrown in the pig bucket. I remember how incensed Addle was over the episode. 'It just shows how careless farmers are,' he said, 'not to examine their pigs' food properly. Or if he did examine it, to feed his pigs on silk embroidery is nothing short of criminal.' I cannot help taking the more feminine view of regret for the loss of the treasure. The curious thing is that the prophecy of the couplet came true, for when young Simon Trespass grew up he became an interior decorator and never married.

Before I leave the subject of pigs and go on to other live stock, I feel I must tell you one or two useful hints, culled from Addle's experience, with little additions of my own.

(1) Pigs are very susceptible to draughts. An old stocking tied round their neck, or a comforter knitted from non-coupon wool especially whilst farrowing, is much appreciated.

(2) Pigs like a shovel full of cinders in their sty, to munch. Addle says this is for teeth cleaning purposes. If that is so, surely the addition of some carbolic tooth powder, or even a little scouring powder, would be a good thing? But Addle says I must try it first on some-one else's pigs.

(3) Pigs love to rootle—that is to dig in the ground, for artichokes, truffles, etc. Put them to do this in the autumn in a place where you afterwards want to plant bulbs, and you will save yourself quite a lot of labour.

I must end with a story about rootling, which is, I am quite aware, rather against myself, but luckily a sense of humour was one of the gifts which the good fairies did *not* leave out at my Christening. Here goes then.

We had decided—one day not long before the war, it was—to kill a pig, somewhat to Addle's regret, as the sow in question, Bengers Belle, had taken many prizes and was a great favourite with my husband. But he never let sentiment interfere with bacon. Accordingly he went down to the farm after breakfast to supervise the killing with Chutney, our head man. The pigs had all been turned out in one of the orchards for several days, and on this particular morning, every one seemed to be present except Bengers Belle, who appeared to have strayed. I was otherwise engaged at the time, so only heard the story afterwards. Apparently Addle and Chutney searched every orchard, and finally the garden itself. Suddenly Chutney, shading his eyes with one hand, exclaimed:

'There she is, m'lord, over on the other side of that hedge.'

The following conversation then ensued:

Addle.   Where?   I can't see her.

Chutney.   Look, m'lord, over there, in her ladyship's water garden.   There—she moved.   Do you see her?

Addle.   Can't see a thing.

They advanced stealthily, in case Bengers Belle took fright. Then Chutney said:

Look, m'lord, you must see her now, next to that patch of yellow irises.   She'll be rootling for bulbs, I reckon.

Addle.   What?   Oh, yes, I can see her now.

(They came closer.)

Chutney.   Now we've got her, m'lord.   I'll stay here, if your lordship will cut her off the other end.

Addle (as they closed in).   You fool, Chutney.   That's not a sow, it's only her ladyship!

It was quite true! I had been bending down, in a pale pink dress, planting some new irises. Poor Chutney was so overcome with horror that he just bolted for home, but Addle was really rather annoyed. 'Damn the fellow,' he said. 'Now we shall have to start looking for Bengers Belle all over again.'

XII

CHEERFUL COCKS AND HAPPY HENS

I HAVE already told my dear readers that my husband has never been keen on poultry, which seems all wrong when one comes to think that the family name is McClutch, and indeed they were the originators of the once famous Caledonian Buffs, every one of which was unfortunately (though patriotically) killed in 1902 on the occasion of King Edward VII's coming to lunch at Castle Eigg, so there is now no trace of the splendid breed. But apart from that, I feel I am in a position of some authority on the subject, on account of my second son, Hector, who has gone in for poultry-keeping on a very large scale, and knows more about it than any man in England probably, though he has, sad to say, had phenomenally bad luck in his various ventures.

Heccy has suffered, in some ways, a thwarted career. After failing for the army he found—or others found for him—that he was not temperamentally suited to business, the Diplomatic Service or the Bar (to which it is only too true that many are called but few are chosen); so there seemed nothing for it but Politics, and accordingly he stood, unsuccessfully for two by-elections, and finally with success for North Bucks. Unluckily though, he never had a good memory for names, and the fact of his referring, at three important meetings and once in the House, to his constituency as North Berks created, I fear, a bad impression, and in the election of 1931 he lost his seat. It was then that he decided to renounce Politics and enter the poultry world. He felt that his experience in swaying and gaining the sympathy of con-stituents could be used with just as good effect—possibly more—on chickens. In 1932 therefore, Addle gave him £5,000 to set him up as a wholesale poultry-keeper.

I forgot to say that he had married, five years previously, Barge Gore-Blymigh,[1] daughter of one of our oldest friends, so the marriage gave us great pleasure, apart from the joy of having Barge herself, who is one of those splendid people, big in every way, who make the world a better place. She was not really suited to the public life of a Member's wife—apart from anything else no photographer ever managed to get the whole of her into one picture—but we felt sure that farming was the life for her, and indeed so it proved. There was some-thing strong and protecting about her that seemed to appeal to the fowls at once. To see the baby chicks run to her instinctively and nestle under her skirts when she crouched down was a touching sight indeed.

Of course the two young people made mistakes at the outset, as all novices are apt to do. When the first lot of 250 day-old chicks arrived a week before the food for them was due to be delivered, and in spite of Heccy and Barge essaying to feed each one by hand with porridge out of George III coffee spoons, the majority died, it was very disappointing. Another time a new lot were given castor oil by mistake for cod liver oil in their food, which made them extremely ill. Then Heccy got Red Mite, and once Barge got shut into the incubator all night. Poor girl, she went down to twelve stone after that dreadful experience.

But sooner or later, with more capital supplied by Addle, the chicken farm settled down into working order, though it never at any time made a profit. Still, as Heccy

Lady Margery Gore-Blymigh, 14th daughter of the Duke of Strewth.

said, any farmer can make money but it takes real knowledge to keep chickens happy, and he concentrated on making it a kind of Hens' Ideal Home, where experiments in breeding and other problems could be practised without discomfort to the inmates. He made great strides in the cause of science, and the fact that no other farmers have taken up his ideas is a reflection on their intelligence, not on Heccy's.

One of his inventions is what he calls the McClutch Psychiatry Test for sex-determination (I do not like using that first word, but am told there is no other and that it is an accepted phrase) of young chicks. (There are several existing tests, one of them invented by the Japs, which claims to determine what I mentioned before at one day old, but as Heccy says, after Pearl Harbour, how can we trust it?) My son's method is done by bits of looking-glass and ribbon and ping-pong balls. Put the chicks amongst these things, he declares, and the baby pullets will naturally go to look at themselves in the mirrors and play with the finery, while the little cockerels will nose the balls about. Heccy has had a 30 per cent success with the idea already, which surely proves its soundness in outline, though it is not perfect yet, he admits.

Another trouble with all poultry-keepers is the hen which goes broody when you don't want her to. Heccy read in an article somewhere that a hen's temperature always rises when she is broody. Accordingly he designed, and Addle gave him the money to have carried out, a kind of bellows which can be quickly and easily slipped under the sitting hen, thus creating an under draught, which cures broodiness instantly. Unfortunately the first design was a little drastic and many of the birds got severe chills and died, but again, Heccy counts on his father helping him with another, gentler model.

But of course the final problem is egg production. Every possible method has been tried by farmers all over the world for this—making their hens jump for food, restricting their exercise, giving them various spices and so on. Heccy says they are all on the wrong tack, and again, his political training has stood him in good stead. Make a hen happy, he maintains, give her social security and freedom from worry, and her one desire, just as with human beings, will be to fulfil herself and lay plenteous eggs. He therefore solemnly promises them extra food and better housing and chick conditions when they have achieved a certain quota of eggs, and he is convinced, except for a few hopelessly stupid birds, that they will respond to the idea after the war, when there are fewer aircraft overhead to upset them. He is also planning to have music relaid to all the hen houses so as to promote contentment, but of course this will entail a fair amount of expense, and oddly enough Addle, who is the soul of generosity, is suddenly jibbing at the cost. He even suggested the other day that Heccy should abandon poultry farming and try his hand at bee-keeping. 'My dear Addle,' I said in surprise, 'you know that is impossible. Can you have forgotten 1889 so quickly?'

For though we never speak of it, there is a strange and tragic story connected with bee-keeping in our family. My beloved mother was a very keen apiarist, and always insisted on taking the honey herself, saying that the bees knew she loved them and would never sting her, especially when she wore her veil, rubber gloves and high boots. Mipsie seemed to inherit this affection—she often said that the life of a Queen Bee was the most perfect in Nature—and she firmly believed in the old adage of 'telling the bees', and would spend much of her time in the Apiary, murmuring her innocent girl-hood's secrets into their sympathetic golden ears.

One day, when she had just come back from a house-party for Cowes Regatta, I noticed that she seemed restless and preoccupied. Observing her with sisterly affection, I said, half teasing, half seriously: 'You had better go and tell the bees, darling, whatever it is.' To my surprise Mipsie jumped up instantly: 'You're right, Blanche, I will,' she said, and ran out of the room.

I never knew what it was my beautiful sister 'told the bees' that evening, but next morning the whole family of six hives were found dead—of Isle of Wight disease.

I wrote this poem for Heccy and Barge's dear little girl Bungie (Barbara), who is particularly fond of the good things of life and has now, poor mite, to be denied them.

PRIVATION

Sleep, my child; I cannot give thee
Cream with cereals any more.
Thou must live without bananas
For alas, we are at war.
We must bravely face the rations
And the other woes in store.
    Sleep, my darling, sleep and rest.
    The Minister of Food knows best.

Mother, where are all the grouse gone?
Why no buttered shrimps of late?
It's so long, dear Mother, since I
Saw *creme brulée* on my plate.
Ah, my child, baked beans thy lot now,
Marge thy burden, spam thy fate.
    Sleep, my darling, sleep and rest.
    The Minister of Food knows best.

Mother, can't we make some toffee,
As we did in days gone by?
I have had no sweets since Monday—
Give me coupons or I'll die.
No, my treasure. (Oh, what anguish
One's own offspring to deny)
    Sleep, my darling, sleep and rest.
    The Minister of Food knows best.

Mother, when the war is over,
Will the world once more be gay?
Will there be an end of horrors,
Fruitless cakes and loaves of grey?
Shall I over-eat at parties
And be sick on Christmas Day?
Sleep, my darling, sleep and rest
The Minister of Food knows best.

XIII

GREEN FRIENDS

As the great Lord Salisbury once said to me, with that profoundness of thought that was part of his genius, there is nothing so attractive as a kitchen garden.

I was of course showing him our own at Coots Balder, which was without doubt one of the most beautiful and original ones in England. All the vegetables were invariably planted, I remember, in *straight rows*, while every bed was bordered by tiny box hedges, each one lovingly clipped *by hand* by our splendid staff of devoted gardeners. Round the entire garden went a magnificent high brick wall, with—at the four corners and over each entrance—the simple dignity of a lone stone coot. It was a very fine sight.

But more of gardens anon. To-day's letter must be devoted to vegetable cookery.

First, however, let me say something in tribute to my dear friend, Bee Cracknell,[1] whose sad death occurred so recently. She was a staunch vegetarian, and indeed something of a scientific pioneer, for she claimed to have discovered a new force called Vitamin Q, which had been undetected hitherto because it has absolutely no effect in any direction whatsoever—but Bee said she always *felt* it was there all the time. She was also a leader in vegetarian wear, especially charcoal shoes, lichen fur coats and underclothes woven of the finest seisal, so as to avoid causing any psychological and spiritual depression to the robbed silkworm.

Yet there was nothing of the crank about Bee, and she was the jolliest person imaginable. When I remarked on this one day she replied: 'Do you know why I am so

[1] Lady Beatrice Cracknell.

jolly? Because I swallow seven raw jumping beans
every morning. They are the secret of internal perpetual
motion, keeping one's liver in perfect condition.'

It seems tragic to think that only a few short weeks
elapsed before I was sent for to see poor Bee on her
death-bed. Her face was ravaged by grief and she
looked a broken woman. In whispers she told me her
awful news. She had just found out that Jumping
Beans jumped because a small maggot—from some
very underhand motive surely—lived inside them. For
years therefore she had been eating flesh unwittingly.
The shock brought about the stroke from which she
died—a martyr to her belief if ever there was one.

Though I admire these brave chemists who discover
pillories and talcum and all those wonderful things in our
daily fare, I cannot say I really understand the scientific
side of food yet, though I intend to master it when I have
a moment to spare. I am, however, a very strong
believer in the properties that exist in Mother Earth, and
personally, I consider that vegetables should never be
washed before cooking. Does a sheep wash the turf
before he crops it? Or a dog remove the mould from
his muzzle before eating his dinner? No. Then who
are we to improve on Nature's ways?

This theory of mine reminds me of a pretty story concerning two of our evacuees, one of which I have already
mentioned in these pages—little Gary Briggs. The other,
Marlene Ruddock, is about the same age, and the two are
firm friends and often exchange remarks at meals about
their innocent little ploys which we grown-ups don't
attempt to understand. I was somewhat surprised the
other day, however, when we were eating a parsnip and
cocoa mould (a speciality of my own), to see Marlene
stare at her plate and then say, 'Six.' Gary replied,
'Five,' upon which Marlene said with some heat, 'That's

MY BROTHER HUMPO IN AN EARLY REEL

a lie. You're five. I'm six.' Both children then caught
my inquiring glance, blushed and became silent.

It all seemed very mysterious, for as they were both
seven years old it was unlikely that they could have been
discussing their relative ages, so after lunch I followed
them to inquire into the secret. And what did I find?
The dear creatures had been collecting objects which they
had found in the food at Bengers. Gary had four
pebbles, a piece of straw and an earwig; Marlene three
pebbles, a drawing-pin and two clothes moths. (They
had tied!) I felt rather ashamed of the clothes moths, but
delighted to think I had started these little Londoners on
Nature Study, and I have given them some beautiful
mahogany collecting cases which Addle had as a boy for
birds' eggs, and told them I will do my best to provide
them with more specimens.

I must close with a word about salads. I have, I
trust, made it abundantly clear that, in my belief, it is
for us women—no matter what class (only last week I
had quite a long talk with the daughter of a New Year
Honour), to help our country by food economy whenever
possible. I believe there was a fashion not long ago for
something called 'the Hay Diet'—though I think perhaps
to feed on nothing but hay is a little extreme. But don't
be afraid of experiments. Dandelions have long been
used in salads—very well, then, try grounsel, plantain,
or fresh lawn mowings. If your evacuees are ill or leave
it is Hitler's fault for making such substitutes necessary.
Just one word of advice, however. If you still have
servants they are better suited by a more conventional
salad of lettuce, cucumber, tomato and hard-boiled egg.

French dressing can still be achieved quite successfully
by substituting linseed for olive oil, or making love to
your garage proprietor, and getting him to give you just a
teacupful of oil from some place he calls 'the sump'.

XIV

HERBS AND SIMPLES

How the very mention of herbs wafts one back over the centuries, to the days of pomades, balms, unguents and even potions!

This last recalls a romantic story of my own family. The history really starts with the wife of the second Earl Coot, Lady Flora O'Flynn that was. Fey Flora she was called, and very lovely she must have been, by all accounts, with her long pale face and tall figure. (A picture of her, in shocking condition—the picture of course I mean—used to hang in the hall at Coots Balder, called 'The White Horse'. It was recently cleaned and proved to be a portrait of Flora, Countess Coot.)

Anyway, she was very interested in spells and potions, having been, I believe, at a convent with Madame de Brinvilliers, and her diary of 1659 records the fact that she 'cured her husband of the virtuous but melancholy habit of reciting the Book of Numbers in his sleepe, by myxing a potion of horehound and pokeweed juice, together with a rare herb knowne as bedsittany.'

Now comes the strange part. A brother of my fathers, Uncle Iggy,[1] developed the same strange inclination, especially after an evening spent at his club, when he would recite in his sleep, it is said, whole pages of Scott, or more frequently of Ruff's Guide to the Turf. It was this last that most troubled my aunt, who was somewhat straight-laced, and she resolved to try the potion which had been used by her husband's ancestress so successfully.

Unfortunately, Uncle Iggy had been equally troubled

[1] Col. The Hon. Ignatius Coot.

by Aunt Katie's constant disapproval of his late nights, and accordingly had trained a parrot to recite, so that— in the dark—his absence from the bedroom would not be noted. And it happened that the fateful night of the potion—which she slipped in to his nightcap without his knowledge—was also the fateful night when Uncle Iggy at last considered the parrot to be able to sustain his part.

Alas, for the best laid of human plans! For some reason the bird—being perhaps a little nervous at his first performance—completely forgot himself, and instead of reciting Lord Shaftsbury's report on the Sweated Labour commission, uttered a shrill squawk and cried 'Scratch a poll'. Poor Aunt Katie screamed loudly and lit a candle. There, shrouded in her husband's night-shirt, was a live parrot. What could she do but assume that she had used the wrong potion and transformed Uncle Iggy, and for the rest of her life she continued to believe this, and to treat her husband as an impostor.

I remember seeing Aunt Kate once when I was about ten; a gracious, happy old lady, quietly reading the Church Times to the parrot, who was, apparently, a far more docile and receptive listener than my uncle had ever been. So the story has a happy ending.

There is indeed something almost magic about herbs, and before the war I used to have my own little herb patch like any cottage woman, which I kept well stocked with rare and fragrant specimens by sending my head gardener on a month's tour of the herb specialists each year. I often used to send little packets or bottled tisanes made from old recipes, to my friends for their ailments. Here are some of them:

False Mugflax and Sissiegrass. For flat feet.
The oil of *Giant Knight's Honour* with a little pounded

Shrift (pluck your shrift as short as possible). For low spirits after 'flu or other setbacks.

Medico Bane (picturesquely known in Hertfordshire, from its flexible fronds as *Doctor's Fingers*). Sovereign remedy for swollen ankles.

Dried *Auntsrue* mixed with distilled *Hassock*. For a gritty skin.

Tansy. For quinsy.

There are also of course many delightful herbs which can be used in cooking, besides the well-known varieties; especially *Common Dame*, which rears its head well above the height of a man, *Scribe's Prattle*, which likes to be planted in a shady situation, and *Maiden's Padlock*, which is however very difficult to obtain, and only has a short season. Sometimes I try making a soup of all the herbs in my garden—a sprig of each—which I chop up and boil into a bouillon. If it still lacks flavour and substance I add a little chutney or guava jelly.

Sad to say some of these lovely things have had to make way for more useful commodities in war-time, and I have pulled up the whole of Abercorn and Grafton (I called each bed after a ducal friend and bordered it with strawberry leaves) to make way for woad, as I felt I could help my country by dyeing little things myself, and saving the overworked cleaners. My first attempt, however, was somewhat marred by an untoward incident.

I had mixed my woad—after several experiments—and taken up a basin full of the rich blue liquid to my bathroom, where I left it on a chair while I went to fetch some cushion covers which I thought needed a little refreshing in colour. Something delayed me, and on my return I found to my horror that Addle, for some unknown reason, had elected to go upstairs and change for dinner half an hour earlier than usual. Furthermore, he had, after his bath, suddenly adopted an old Turkish

Bath habit of sitting down with the evening paper.   The
result was very unlucky indeed, though I tried to comfort
him by comparing him to the ancient Britons.   But
Addle is strangely sensitive about some things.   'Ancient
baboon, you mean,' I heard him mutter as he went into
his dressing-room, and I left it at that, feeling the whole
thing was perhaps something which only time could efface.

I forgot to mention, when discussing my herb garden,
that Mipsie fervently believes in *Rapesbane* as a pick-
me-up.   Poor darling, she has sorely needed one lately,
her health never having quite recovered from the shock
of the fall of the South of France.

XV

SWEETS TO THE SWEET

In these drab and dreary war-time days it is pleasant indeed to let the mind dwell on the gay, colourful, almost fairy-tale quality of sweets.

I have always craved beauty in any form, as men crave heady wine. In early nursery days Mipsie and I would lie, like two lawless poachers, regardless of exposure and discomfort, on the pile carpet of the top landing at home, watching with breathless interest the brilliant and gracious guests go down to dinner four floors below. Shimmering satin and sparkling jewels!

'Aren't they beautiful, Mipsie?' I whispered to her once.

'Yes, lovely, Blanchie,' she replied, 'especially the ones with long moustaches.' I had been looking at the women, she at the men!

Later in life, when I was shown my new governess, I am told I shrieked out, 'Take her away, take her away, she's ugly!' Mama then took me aside and gently explained that governesses had to be plain, for reasons which she said I should understand later. But I digress.

What sweets they were in those wonderful old days! Great towering edifices of the pastry cook's art, sometimes several feet high. There was one occasion, I recall, when my father permitted his coronet to be modeled (with two detectives standing by in case of accidents) in puff pastry and wine-coloured ice cream. Another time when the chef whom I mentioned earlier in these pages had set his heart on an exact replica of the Eiffel Tower in angelica, filled with bon-bons, for some special occasion. Being an artist to his finger tips, he told my mother that he must be sent over to Paris for the week-end in order to refresh his memory. 'Nonsense,' my father said to Mama, when told of the plan. 'You can't possibly spare him, dear. I will go to Paris instead of chef and bring back a faithful description of the Eiffel Tower.' I tell this little anecdote to show how my father, martinet though we sometimes thought him, yet had his gentle and considerate side.

Indeed, I have reason to remember that visit to Paris for another reason, and one that further shows Papa's loving disposition, which was hidden so deeply under the aristocrat's iron reserve. Shortly after he returned, the butler entered the drawing-room with a small package, which he had found in a coat pocket when unpacking; a package which proved to be—the most beautiful sapphire bracelet imaginable. Inside the case was a slip of paper bearing these words: 'à Mademoiselle Blanche, avec mille remerciements de son ami devoué, COOT.'

Needless to say I jumped up, clapping my hands, and seized on my treasure. I remember crying, 'But Papa, why a present to *me* suddenly, and why call me Mademoiselle and not sign yourself Papa, and why write in French, and *thank* me, and why not give me the present before?' But Papa only pinched my cheek and told me not to ask so many questions but to make the most of my luck, which I certainly did. Papa seemed, truth to tell, really put out that the existence of the bracelet had slipped his memory till that moment. What beautiful manners from a father to a daughter!

To return to sweets, I have always said that the menu is half the battle. Read that you are eating Zabaglione, and you will expect Zabaglione. That is why I stick to menus—though for paper economy I cut up sugar cartons and stick them in our lovely silver holders— and that is why I was able proudly to announce on it the other day 'Banana Melba with whipped cream.' Let me tell you how it was done. For my banana, I cut out a turnip in *precisely* the same shape, covered it in custard, and made an exquisite 'top dressing' consisting of a pint of dried milk, sweetened with saccharine, to which I added a tube of one of the best and purest makes of tooth-paste, which whipped like a dream, and tasted faintly of peppermint, an added advantage as it disguised the fact that the turnip did not taste of banana. What could be simpler?

Another useful and harmless deception is Blackcurrant Charlotte—which to the initiated is really Sago Charlotte, made with stale bread and sago died with very strong cochineal. If you want to complete the picture you can scatter in a few finely-chopped flower stalks which look like the stalks of the blackcurrants and deceive any but the most discerning eye. Unluckily, my evacuees all possess that sharp intelligence which is so often found in the dear old cockney folk.

One last piece of advice, touching pastry. It is always wisest to have not only a very sharp knife, but a bread saw as well when serving. Sometimes, however, I find a pastry is still stubborn and resists all efforts. When this occurs try this recipe.

Grate the hard remains and soak them overnight in the rinsing water from a used jam or marmalade jar. Next day, take your pastry pulp and work it into a flan shape, which you fill with any remnants handy. Some cereals, the end of a pudding, a piece of stale cake or crumpet perhaps. Sweeten a white sauce with sugar beet, pour over the top and bake quickly. The result is really very tasty, considering, and extremely economical. I call it White Elephant Flan, and intend to present one to our Salute the Soldier Fête, of which I shall tell you more next week.

THE MOSS ROSE

(My mother was passionately attached to moss roses, as the charming little poem which is given here will show.)

A little pink rosebud, folded neat
Was plucked one day, as a special treat,
For a bridesmaid's bouquet gay.
But quite overcome by the honour great
(For the bridegroom was heir to a marquisate),
She blushed the live-long day.

'Supposing my petals brown,' she said,
'And supposing I can't keep up my head,
I shall just disgrace them all.
The bold carnations are used to this,
And those dreadful orchids would think it bliss,
But for me, I am far too small.'

They arrived at St. George's, Hanover Square,
And so many splendid folk were there
That she shook like a wind blown plant.
When she suddenly saw that the bride's own face
Was screened by a veil of Brussels lace
(Lent by the bridegroom's aunt).

'Ah me,' the little pink rosebud cried,
'If even a lovely (and titled) bride
Is permitted to veil her face;
Then surely the same should be granted to me.
Oh Fairies, list to my prayer,' said she,
'And give me a veil of lace.'

As the rosebud was slumbering, still quite tight,
In a priceless cut glass vase that night
(The gift of the Duke of Quorn),
The Fairies threw o'er her tired wee face
An exquisite veil of Nature's lace—
And that's how the Moss Rose was born.

XVI

A FÊTEFUL DAY

ALTHOUGH I am so tired that I can scarcely hold the pen, I realize with what interest and affection my beloved Public follow my movements and await my weekly advice, and know that they will rejoice to hear that our Salute the Soldier Fête in Bengers Great Park last Saturday was an outstanding success.

From its first inception originality was my aim. 'I want everything to be different this time,' I told my committee. 'People are tired of the same old stalls and side-shows. We must strike not only a new note, but a whole vibrant chord of novelty.'

My committee are all splendid folk, but a little lacking in initiative, and in the end all the suggestions came from me. They were carried unanimously, however, by all except my close neighbour and friend Daisy de Grubbe, who objected to so many things at the first meeting that I did not send her notices of the subsequent ones. Daisy is a dear girl—I have known her since we both came to Hertfordshire as brides fifty-two years ago—but she is sadly unco-operative in matters of this kind, and I feel strongly in these perilous days that 'those that are not for us are against us.'

The weather however *was* with us luckily, and Mipsie arrived to open proceedings looking lovely as usual in a delightful new chrome yellow dress—at least it looked new, but she swore it was several days old, and that it was the first time she had ever been forced to open a fête in a worn frock, or come from London in a hired

car, not her own Rolls. What hardships war brings to
us all.

After her speech, I arranged for five small school
children, dressed as rations (in paper dresses to save
material, with cardboard hats to save paper) to recite
a little opening poem, which I wrote specially for the
occasion. There were eighteen verses, of which I give
the first as a sample:

> We rations do salute the soldiers brave,
> And strive our bit to do their lives to save.
> For lo! we also bear of war the brunt,
> 'Cos we are allies of the kitchen front.

After that came an eager inspection of the many gay
stalls and side-shows, which included my innovation of a
Bring and Fry Sale—whereat everyone had to bring some
raw materials and cook and auction them in front of a
delighted crowd of spectators. Many hung back from
shyness though, so in the end I did most of it myself. But
the village people bid splendidly for my wares, dear
good creatures that they are, though it was sad that nearly
all of them left their purchases behind—in the excitement
of the day, no doubt.

For side-shows, we had such frivolities as Aunt Sally
(only called Aunty Beany, because we had tins of baked
beans instead of clay pipes), Bowling for an Egg, and
Guessing Addle's Weight. What a time I had getting
him to consent to it too, and he only gave way in the
end on condition that I let him off the next item, namely
the Comic Husband Show.

This is run, in case any other fêtes wish to copy us,
exactly the same as a comic dog show, with different
heats for the most handsome husband, the fattest
husband, the fastest husband (they had to run for razor

blades), the best-kept husband, and so on. The only pity was that there were so few entries, and for the husband with the most sentimental eyes, which I thought would be a riotous success, not one single man was entered. I fear there is much truth in the adage that Englishmen take their pleasures sadly.

Tea was run very successfully, as usual, by our Institute, the public having to bring their own eatables, sugar, milk, cup and plate. In compliment to our gallant allies, I had put up over the little enclosure 'TEA—the order of the day', and all the helpers were in Russian costume, with our vicar's wife looking splendid as Stalin. How we laughed too when her enormous moustache fell off into a full can of tea!

And after tea came my Treasure Hunt.

I call it mine, because not only was the idea and organization all mine, but I also found and in a sense gave the treasure. A real live treasure, too, in the form of an excellent maid, exempt from national service on account of being stone deaf, with a bad impediment in her speech, who doesn't mind where she goes! I thought her salary of £3 a week a trifle high, so guaranteed half out of my own pocket for three months, which is as long as anyone would expect to keep a maid these days. And I installed her in an easy chair in the azalea grove, with a good supply of illustrated papers, a radio, and fifty cigarettes, as she told me she was a chain smoker.

Tickets were 5s. each, and we had 158 entries! They had to follow clues, of course, planned and also written in rhyme by me. And such was the excitement aroused by the event that most of the fête visitors followed the hunt as well, and even I felt I must 'be in at the death,' so took a short cut to the place where I had hidden my treasure.

To my horror she was gone!

There was the radio still going beside an empty chair and an empty box of cigarettes. I looked frantically for my plan of the hunt, then remembered I had given it to Mipsie to take care of, as I am always so stupid dropping things about. I waited till most of the competitors had arrived, and then explained that something must have gone wrong and conducted them all back to the house.

And there, seated on the terrace, smoking contentedly, we found the Treasure with Mipsie, who with her usual quickness had beaten the whole hunt, and 'found' several minutes before I arrived on the spot.

I was overjoyed to think my own sister had won the prize, and very angry with several people who hinted that Mipsie had never entered for the hunt at all. The world is a harsh place, I often think, and women will always say unkind things about a famous beauty.

XVII

A SAVOURIE DYSSHE

Where would England be, I often think, without her savouries? Angels on Horseback, Scotch Woodcock, Cheese Straws. As typical of English simplicity and charm as wild roses or boiled cabbage. People talk about the Eton Wall game being won on the platforms of Waterloo, but it is equally true that the great English houses were kept up in the past by the aid of low taxation and a constant supply of welsh rarebit in the servants' hall.

Of course, that particular dish was quite taboo in the upper classes then. I well remember, as a child, choosing it for a birthday lunch (attracted by its name perhaps, for I could certainly never have tasted it) and being told by Nannie to select something more suitable for a little lady. Nevertheless, a great-uncle of mine, Lord Algernon Twynge, had a peculiar penchant for welsh rarebit, and every evening, after his wife had retired, he slipped through the baize door to the servants' quarters, apparently, and indulged in his secret vice in the housekeeper's room with the cook and the butler. His low tastes eventually led him to disaster however, for after his wife's death he married the cook, and the pair thereafter indulged together far into the night, sometimes consuming as many as eight or nine welsh rarebits on end, I believe.

How times have changed since then! Class prejudices have largely vanished, which I think myself is a good thing, at any rate with regard to welsh rarebits. And before we leave the subject I would like to tell my readers of a little fancy of mine, which they may care to copy. If your melted cheese turns out very stringy, as it often does, don't grumble, but make a virtue of its stringiness by winding it round potato balls, sticking two knitting needles in each ball, and quickly altering the menu to 'Cheese Worsted Balls.' It makes a gay interlude in the meal.

Gaiety, I think, is so important in life, even in the kitchen. I always make a point of singing while I am preparing a dish, especially with something rather tedious like cake-making, or grating cheese. Which latter, by the way, caused us all to have a good laugh the other day.

I was cooking a macaroni au gratin, and being in an economical mood, was having a good clear up of all the ends of cheese I could find, and grating little bits till my fingers ached. So to cheer myself on I sang right through 'Green grow the rushes-o" and 'One man went to mow'—two old favourites of mine—so that I quite forgot my tiresome occupation, and by the time I reached the last verse there was a lovely big pile of cheese!

We were very gay at dinner that night (when Addle is out I always have it with my evacuees), and I was amusing them with various recollections of monarchs, and some of the funny things that happened at court balls, when suddenly, I noticed that they had all stopped eating, and that I was the only one partaking of the macaroni cheese. 'Now, my dear good people, you mustn't get so interested that you don't eat,' I started to say, but to my horror, as I spoke the words, I discovered myself to be foaming at the mouth! Little Marlene Ruddock cried out 'She's mad! Mum, Lady Addle's mad!' and ran screaming from the room. It was only then that we realized— though my evacuees said they had suspected it earlier from the taste—that I had grated up some remnants of household soap with my cheese!

All that is needed for a good savoury, I have often said, is a little toast and a lot of imagination—or some-times a lot of imagination and a lot of toast, as in the case

H.H. ARCHDUKE BLOTTO OF LOTHARIA

of one of my specialities which I call 'Toast sur toast' (it sounds so much more attractive in French), which is a useful dish for breakfast left-overs, being simply layers of toast spread with different things in turn, one layer fish paste, one cheese, one chutney or pickles, etc. Get as many flavours as you can and then make your guests try to guess them, and it becomes a good parlour game as well as a course.

Another handy savoury is stuffed buns or scones, when you have any stale ones to use up. Cut your bun in half, and scoop out the inside. Next do likewise with a beetroot or large carrot, leaving only an empty shell. Now chop up your vegetable, season it, and stuff your bun, popping it into a quick oven for ten minutes or so. The great thing about this savoury is that you can then use the middle of the bun or scone for stuffing the beet or carrot. Call one dish 'Petit pains farci' and the other 'Betrave au petit pain' and keep up a reputation for variety of menu.

These two little examples show how one's individuality can and should be stamped on one's home, even in cookery. And I cannot resist telling the compliment I was paid not long ago by a distinguished Frenchman whom we put up for the night. It was my evening for cooking, and I took special pains with the dinner, giving him four courses of my most varied dishes. He was evidently impressed, because he asked, later in the evening, who cooked for me. Smiling, I answered, 'All my own work, monsieur, as the pavement artist states.' He bowed, also smiling. 'Ah, madame, but unlike the pavement artist, the impression of your cooking lingers on,' he said courteously.

Coming from one of a nation of *bon viveurs*, I shall always treasure that remark.

XVIII

THREE VISITORS

I FEEL as excited as a girl as I write to-day's letter, because two wonderful things are about to happen. First and foremost, my dear Margaret is coming on leave and bringing with her—what do you think? A Polish officer! Secondly, my dear Mipsie is giving up her London flat and coming to stay at Bengers indefinitely, which is truly delightful.

The name of her friend, so Margaret writes, is Lieut. Radowczki, and I at once telephoned to a cousin who knows one of the stenographers in the Polish Embassy, to ask her to find out something about his family. It seems he is quite *bien*, though not a member of one of the best families, and is also financially ruined, but one can't have everything. Margaret has never brought a young man to the house before. I told my readers of the tragedy of Billy Bynde-Wede. There was another charming young man in 1942 who rang her up one day, but it transpired that he had only met Margaret once before, in a very dark air-raid shelter, and the friendship, alas, came to nothing. So it will be understood how excited I am at this new development, and how determined to bring matters to a satisfactory conclusion if humanly possible.

As for Mipsie, I fear she has undergone another of those bitter experiences of which she has had her full share in life, poor darling. It will be remembered that I organized a Treasure Hunt at our fête, and helped to provide the treasure—in the form of a real live maid—myself, by guaranteeing her wages of £3 a week. Mipsie won her, to my great joy, in spite of one or two nasty things people said about the episode, and took her back to London. For a fortnight it worked perfectly—then Mipsie found out that the maid was drawing £3 a week from her as well as 30s. from me! It was a great shock to her to think of anyone behaving so dishonourably. With her beauty and charm she has never been accustomed to being crossed in anything, and now, when the autumn of her life draws near, she has —as I heard one of my evacuees sympathetically put it— been double-crossed. What picturesque and telling expressions some of the lower classes do have to be sure.

So of course I have been busy all day preparing a right royal welcome for my guests. Mipsie, I know, never minds what she eats so long as it's anything out of season. So I managed to get some oysters which as there is no R in the month may be unreliable, so I think will be better as oyster soup (a tin of potato soup with the oysters popped in at the last moment) and was also lucky enough to get a few fresh peaches, from my fishmonger who got them through his barber's insurance agent. Having got thus far with the dinner I turned my attention to Margaret. What would my dear girl like best? Assuredly, I decided, she would wish a compliment paid to her young man by one of his national dishes?

I have always been interested in foreign cookery, but have not attempted any dishes from my International Cookery Book since one of my evacuees had rather a bad choking fit from some birdsnest soup which I must somehow have got a little wrong. (I always read up the recipe and then do my own version of it, as I feel it is then less stereotyped.) But I got out the book again to-day and studied *Bigos*, which is a truly national Polish dish, consisting of a kind of sour cabbage pie, which is put back into the oven every day, so that the flavour gets stronger and stronger. I had no time for such a lengthy process, so merely selected the sourest looking cabbage leaves I could find on the silo, and put them, with water and their pastry covering, into the oven all night. This morning the pastry was black and quite hard, which I trust is right. Anyway, the *Bigos* smells *very* strong, which I'm sure will please our gallant guest, as I know foreigners like everything more highly flavoured than do we simple English folk.

I had a little time left before their arrival, so decided to attempt Kol Duny, which are considered a great delicacy in Poland, and are served with the drinks before dinner. Addle is getting out a bottle of vintage sherry, he tells me. Very well, I thought, I will have something worthy of it.

Kol Duny are little pastry balls, stuffed with minced beef and mutton, so my book says. But as we have no meat ration left at this stage of the week, I had to make do with some chopped 'Doggie' (which is probably several kinds of meat mixed together, I thought), only a tinned canine food, it is true, but really not unpalatable, though rather sandy in texture. These I rolled in some paste I had ready made for Addle's press-cutting book— as I had no time to make pastry—and then came the rub, as Shakespeare says. For they are supposed to be boiled, but every time I put one in the boiling water it just disintegrated! It wasn't till I had the bright idea of wrapping each ball in some spare hair nets I had in my bedroom, that I achieved the desired result. Now I am sitting at my desk, alternately typing this and removing the nets from the *Kol duny*. It is a slow business, as the hair nets keep getting entangled in the typewriter keys, and two or three balls have got stained with carbon paper in some way. But I hope soon to be 'all set'.

Kol duny, oyster soup, *bigos*, peaches. It is a dinner fit for a Coot, as my father used to say instead of the usual version. And perhaps—who knows—the last course will be 'Polish officer on toast'—a fiancé for my dear daughter.

XIX

A BITTER DISAPPOINTMENT

ALAS, with what high hopes I wrote last week of my preparations for entertaining my dear Margaret and her Polish officer friend, and my beautiful sister Mipsie. And now when I think how all my plans have come to naught, partly through my fault, or anyway my misfortune I am tempted to say 'bother' very loudly indeed!

They all arrived punctually, Mipsie and Margaret looking delightful as usual, and M. Radowzcki really charming, very handsome with perfect manners. My spirits rose as we assembled for sherry, and of course it was a great asset having Addle there too, as he has an old world courtesy that wins everyone, besides being a splendid conversationalist. 'You from Poland?' I heard him ask Margaret's friend, who replied that he was, and I felt the party was starting off well.

Then came dinner, and at once I realized my grave mistake, which was that oyster soup always brings Margaret out very red and blotchy. I blamed myself bitterly for not starting with Bortch, the deep crimson of which might have made her look pale by comparison.

However, there was nothing to be done, except to pray that M. Radowzcki would not notice. Mipsie tactfully proposed showing him the lake after dinner, for which I was very grateful. I suggested an early bed for Margaret, hoping for great things on the morrow.

But more disasters were to come. One of Margaret's oysters was bad, and the poor child was decidedly ill during the night. She declared that she felt quite recovered by the morning, but Mipsie, who has always been such a devoted aunt, came into her bedroom while I was taking her temperature, and said she thought Margaret looked very white, and should stay in bed till she had got back her colour somewhat.

So I kept her in bed for breakfast, and was delighted to hear the Polish officer expressing great solicitude for her misfortune. But when she descended at about eleven, what was my annoyance to discover M. Radowzcki and Mipsie apparently vanished off the face of the earth! Margaret spent the morning helping her father with his press-cutting book, and just before lunch the wanderers returned. They had got lost in the maze!

'Mipsie, darling,' I chided laughingly. 'You always say you know that maze backwards.'

'I do, Blanche,' she replied, 'but you see I wasn't walking backwards to-day.' As usual, her brilliant wit won the day, and we all roared.

After lunch however I drew her aside and confided my hopes for Margaret, if only we could show her in an attractive light for love's young dream. Mipsie thought for a moment, then suddenly said:

'I know, Blanchie. The swimming pool! Margaret is an excellent swimmer, and so is he, I gather. I will propose a bathe after tea, and he shall see her at her best.'

I wasn't altogether happy about the plan, fearing that a bathing dress didn't make the happiest use of dear Margaret's figure somehow. But I acquiesced, knowing how clever Mipsie always is in worldly matters.

Tea—with real lemon essence in honour of our Polish guest, who I felt sure would drink it the Russian way —was very gay, and afterwards they went up to change. I went to help Margaret arrange her wrap in the wisest manner, and made her promise not to throw it off till just before she dived in. When we reached the swimming pool however, there were Mipsie and M. Radowzcki already dressed for bathing, and to my consternation the young man greeted us with:

'I am to have the honour of teaching Madame the Duchess to swim.'

I was greatly surprised, as I thought Mipsie could swim, but didn't care for bathing. But perhaps, I decided, she felt she could help our little scheme better in the water than on terra cotta. But after some twenty minutes of tuition, I felt I must take a firm line, so proposed a swimming race between the two young people. This was a great success, and the merry laughter that rang out did one good to hear. Then, suddenly, we were startled by a cry from Mipsie, who was out of her depth, struggling in the water.

'Help!' she gasped. 'Cramp!'

In ten seconds M. Radowzcki was beside her, steering her gently to safety. She nearly fainted when she reached the bank, then managed a brave little smile.

'So silly of me,' she said. 'I should have told you, Blanche. Lemon essence always gives me cramp.'

My remorse at the words may easily be imagined! First the oysters, and now the lemon essence. It seemed like malicious fate. Somehow we, or rather Margaret's friend, got poor Mipsie back to the house and to her room. Gallantly, she insisted on coming down to dine though, and lay on a sofa in the long drawing-room, in a lovely jade green wrap, while M. Radowzcki took her, at her request, each course on a tray.

'I don't want to be a trouble to the servants,' she said, with her usual consideration, as she sipped the Veuve Cliquot which Addle had opened specially for her.

Next morning she left in a hired car, giving M. Radowzcki a lift. I urged her to stay, but she was adamant.

'I can't neglect my work,' she said staunchly. (Mipsie has some very trusted secret job, I don't know what, except that I fancy it has something to do with luxury restaurants.)

Margaret hitch-hiked back to duty, and I was left to my own sad thoughts, which I communicated to Mipsie when she returned from town.

'Don't worry, darling Blanche,' she said consolingly, 'he wouldn't do for Margaret. I lunched with him, and, my dear, his family is beggared!'

'But if he's nice, Mipsie,' I argued, 'money isn't everything, and he seemed such a good young man.'

Mipsie shrugged her shoulders.

'Good for one lunch,' she murmured bitterly.

I said no more. Evidently my dear sister found M. Radowzcki in some way lacking in stability of character, and thought him unworthy of Margaret.

So perhaps everything is for the best after all.

MY MOTHER'S MAXIMS

My dear mother used to keep a book (beautifully covered in puce plush, I remember), compiled from her own experience and innate wisdom, of advice for the Home. It was, indeed, this book that led me to write my little volume of *A Hundred Home Hints*. I quote below a page on Entertaining, which seems apposite to my last letter:

A guest should always leave, after a week-end visit, by the earliest train convenient to her host and hostess. Should he or she fail to do this, it is sometimes a good plan for one of the carriage horses that takes them to the station to break a trace, thereby causing them to miss their train. The next visit the guest pays, it will generally be found that he or she selects an earlier train.

If any foreigner should be staying in your house, do not omit to extend to them the same courtesy as you would to one of your own countrymen, endeavouring to express your sympathy in as delicate a manner as possible. There is one pitfall however. Some foreigners are dangerously fascinating. Remember that pity is akin to love.

Never inquire their destination if you should happen to encounter one of your guests in the passages after retiring. Always assume that they are fetching a book from the library and direct them accordingly.

If a lady guest shows signs of ennui or lack of conversation, a hostess should ask her if she has any letters to write before the post leaves, giving her thus the opportunity of going to her room without discourtesy.

If the hostess is herself conscious of the same sensations, she should say to her guests, 'If you will excuse me, I have to see the housekeeper about some jellies for the Almshouse,' or some such politeness indicating her charitable principles. She can then retire to her boudoir with a *couvre pied* and put her feet up for a half-hour's relaxation from social duties.

Never put note-paper bearing a coronet in any guest's bedroom unless you know them well and thoroughly approve their income, way of life and so forth. Visiting governesses should be expected to provide their own note-paper.

XX

MEMORY'S MENU

(1) *Breakfast*

IT has occurred to me that my Public might be interested in my reminiscences of the various meals which play so important a part in our daily lives. Breakfast, lunch, tea, dinner—what memories they conjure up for me! Memories almost too intimate to write of, for have I not shared a dried haddock with a Grand Duke? And toasted a muffin for a Cardinal? As for Mipsie, what has happened to her at various meals in the past would fill a book; but a book, I fancy, locked fast, with a golden key placed near its owner's heart.

Breakfast, I always feel, is of paramount importance in English life. It can make or mar a marriage. Sometimes, indeed, destiny hangs on it. I never read that 'the Cabinet breakfasted at Downing Street' without wishing that the eggs and bacon could know and the marmalade rejoice in the part they had played for their country. It is not a meal suited to proposals of course. Yet I imagine many a mind must have been made up over a house-party breakfast. Perhaps a débutante will descend not looking her best, or with too marked a resemblance to her mother, in the cruel daylight. Perhaps a young man's manners will not stand the test of breakfast after a late Hunt ball. And the course of two people's lives is changed. (I always advised Margaret, if offered breakfast in bed by her hostess, before the war, to accept.)

My dear mother, who possessed such wonderful

wisdom and insight into character, used to say that no two people were exactly the same.   Some, myself included, are at their brightest and best in the morning, and thoroughly enjoy making breakfast a social function. Others, my dear husband amongst them, are sadly different.   'Don't be too optimistic this morning, Blanche,' he sometimes used to say.   'I couldn't bear it.'   For a time I felt this something of a barrier between us, but it was soon bridged by the loving understanding that marriage brings, and I have learnt to sail gaily over Addle's little moods, cheering him up by reading my letters out to him when he is gloomily absorbed in the daily papers.

Another strange case of breakfast being the only fly in a happy marriage is that of our old friend, Lord Gerald Gore-Blymigh, of whom I have written before. 'Gugglie' shared my high spirits in the morning, and used to keep us all in fits of laughter by his witty remarks and ways.   'Cheep, cheep' he would always say when his daily boiled egg was put before him.   Then he would bend down and pretend to hear the chicken inside, while we all, his wife included, doubled up with mirth.   Then suddenly—after sixteen years married bliss—there came a morning when he said 'Cheep, cheep', and instead of laughing she threw her own egg (poached) in his face. No one knew why—whether it was a sudden brain storm— but it ruined their life together.   Gugglie had just lost his seat at that time, and of course a politician's wife should have realized how particularly sensitive—I suppose they would call it allergic nowadays—an ex-M.P. is to any form of eggs in the face.

Talking of breakfast habits reminds me of a distant cousin of Addle's, Sir Henry Hirsute, who insisted on a pair of kippers every morning of his life.   As he lived at Cannes this sometimes presented no little difficulty, and his devoted chef used to spend long hours salting and colouring soles and inserting kipper bones in them. One day, it struck the butler, who always had to remove the bones before Sir Henry started eating, that chef's labour was unnecessary. All that was needed was a plateful of bones on the side table in case their master happened to look there. This deception continued for years, until suddenly it occurred to Sir Henry that the soles did not taste like kippers. Somehow the whole story came out; he dismissed both servants instantly, but in later years appeared to repent of his action, for in his will he left both men a beautiful kipper bone in a glass case, a gold plate affixed to the spine commemorating his employees' devotion.

When I think of breakfast I instinctively turn back over the years to the wonderful meals before the last war, when the footmen groaned beneath the weight of many and varied dishes. Porridge, fishcakes, eggs in several ways, kidneys, sausages, as well as sometimes two enormous hams on the sidetable. Addle says I am always reminding him of the past, but when I think of those old days I find it hard to come down to a weekly egg (if we hadn't our own fowls to keep us plentifully supplied), and imported jam in a tin. Yet at the same time I realize how thankful we should be to our brave merchant seamen and our loyal poultry who make these things possible at all.

There are ways too of varying the breakfast menu, when supplies are short, to avoid the monotony which brings such longing for past glories. I will end with a few wrinkles of my own invention—not the only kind of wrinkles that I possess, I assure you! I have ways of dealing with them too—but more of that anon.

Fishless fishcakes. Get a friend to send you some seaweed, which you put in water with cold cooked potatoes overnight. Make these up into fishcakes in the morning, omitting all but a few particles of seaweed, and they will taste very fishy indeed.

Marmalade without oranges or sugar. Cut in strips the green outside coverings of horse chestnuts and boil till tender. Mix with orange-flavoured cordial and bottle. If too sour, suck a saccharine tablet immediately before use.

To make cereals go further. If you are registered for chickens steal a little balancer meal from your ration and mix it with rolled oats or puffed wheat. If the hens fall off in laying give them one good meal of your cereals to make up. Exchange is no robbery.

(2) *Luncheon*

Perhaps the social revolution which we of the old school have witnessed during the past thirty years is exemplified in luncheon more than in any other function of Society. We have seen our houses turned into flats, even the servants' bedrooms commanding a vast price, and frequented for the first time—except *sub rosa*—by the gentry, we have been forced by super-tax to allow our peers to write for the newspapers and our peeresses to advertise face cream, and for luncheon, one of the most elegant meals of the day, where breeding should count above everything, we have so far deteriorated that only last week I saw a dowager marchioness in a snack bar, and even before the war a terrible innovation called a fork luncheon was beginning to appear in the ranks of the *beau monde*. Indeed, these latter sometimes constituted a positive danger, as I know from Addle, who was not used to such things and heartily disliked them, and who once put his fork right through the hand of an

Italian contessa (she had a very dark skin), thinking it was a cold quail. It quite spoilt his lunch, as he didn't feel like eating the real quail afterwards, and he vowed he would never go to such an unappetizing meal again.

Most serious of all, however, seems to me to be the change in Sunday lunch, which was once the core of family life, the aftermath of mattins, where 'the roast beef of Old England' provided weekly testimony to our country's greatness. What a hive of industry the house would be beforehand too! The gardener would have kept back his best fruit and vegetables for Sunday, the cook and kitchen staff would be about twice as busy as on ordinary days, the butler and footmen, often supplemented by other menservants' in spare uniforms, would be at their smartest, for if anything went wrong with the lunch, woe betide them! My father, indeed, used to say that no gentleman was ever in a good temper for Sunday lunch, and instanced his own father,[1] who used regularly to give one of the servants notice on Sunday in consequence of some shortcoming, either real or imaginary, in the lunch routine. In fact there is a story of him, when he was getting on in life, having turned on his wife in the middle of the night after some Sunday lunch had particularly upset him, and said to her, 'You can go. You are lazy, incompetent and getting past your work,' which so offended Lady Coot that she removed herself to his dressing-room for the remainder of the night.

Nowadays, all is changed. The glory of Sunday lunch has departed. Families still have their joints, it is true, but the meal is beginning to be an easy, somewhat slapdash affair without any special meaning. People—even before the war—had begun to spare their servants. It is sad indeed to think how lax we have grown, as a country, in the keeping of our Sabbath.

[1] 12th Earl Coot.

Other things have departed too, mainly due of course to the war. The cosy lunch-party of ten or a dozen guests, with half as many courses, has completely disappeared. How I used to enjoy these, especially if the party were confined to my own sex, and I could therefore take Margaret with an easy mind, instead of having to keep one eye on her all through lunch to see if the two men placed each side of her were talking to her or not. Usually they would last till the fish course, sometimes to the meat, rarely beyond. Then I would watch first one and then the other turn away and spend the rest of the time conversing with his other neighbour, so that the second half of *my* lunch would have to be spent in making remarks across the table in order to redirect their attention to my daughter. I grew quite adept at this, and several times re-opened the conversation and observed with joy that it lasted right through to the end of lunch; but afterwards, in the drawing-room, they would only drift away somehow, and I would feel that all my labour had been in vain.

Although such functions as these must, of necessity, be restricted in these hard days, yet all the same, by those who still maintain a high standard, a lot can be achieved to-day, as witness my clever sister Mipsie, who contrived to give the most wonderful lunch-party of eighteen not long ago, though with her usual high sense of duty she did not feel justified in doing this in war-time except for a charity, so the lunch was in aid of a firewatchers' dance club in which she was particularly interested.

In case any of my readers want to raise money for a like good cause, I will tell them how she did this.

First, she telephoned or wrote to her many friends, asking them to send her ingredients for the lunch. They responded splendidly, as people always do with her, sending her chickens, salmon, asparagus, melons, etc.

MY MOTHER IN THE HEYDAY OF HER BEAUTY

An exquisite meal was then prepared, to which she invited her smartest friends, charging them only £1 1s. a head, in order to cover the fee of a very attractive young American singer whom she was anxious to support (she is so endlessly kind). Before he sang, however, Mipsie made a touching appeal for the charity, and then took off her own mink hat, like any organ-grinder, and passed it round. Of course £5 and £10 notes showered into it, so that she was easily able to pay for the chef and the wines, and the delightful lunch, therefore, did not cost either her or the charity one penny piece. What it is to be a genius!

(3) *Tea*

My memories of tea will have to be assembled without the help of Mipsie, for the whole subject brings her such nostalgia for Rumpelmeyer's in the Rue de Rivoli— the only place where tea has ever given her real pleasure, otherwise, she says it is a cheap meal—that I hesitate to re-open old wounds. The famous *salle de thé* holds a special romance for her, for it was there that a Russian Prince, after taking her to tea every day for a fortnight, shot himself at her feet because he couldn't pay the bill. "Ah, Blanche,' poor Mipsie said when we were discussing it this morning, 'we shall never see those days again. Nowadays nobody has enough money to do what they can't afford.' I felt the bitter truth in her words, and stole out of the room, leaving her to her sad thoughts.

My first remembrance of tea is sitting in a beautiful Hepplewhite high chair and banging on the tray with an engraved silver spoon. Not, I believe, that I would have cared a fig if it had been plain silver. My worst enemy cannot call me a snob, and I had a healthy appetite in those dear childhood days which rose superior to my

surroundings. Indeed, I recall an occasion when my
father, during one of his bi-annual visits to the nursery,
discovered me and the vicar's daughter innocently eating
off an earthenware doll's tea set, and how furious he was!
'No Coot ought even to be aware that earthenware
exists, 'I remember him saying, as he ordered the
offending tea set to be removed and a china one instantly
bought instead. It was years before I dared to criticize
my father, but now, in the light of modern thought, I
think perhaps his action was a little extreme. I cannot
see why the vicar's daughter should have been forbidden
earthenware.

My next remembrance concerns a cousin of ours,
Mary Twynge,[1] and my younger brother Humpo, who
was an incorrigible practical joker. Mary was always
extremely nervous of insects, and Humpo, knowing this,
would call out, just as she was about to put a piece of
plum cake in her mouth, 'Look out, there's an earwig
on it!' or sometimes he would point to a bit of peel and
swear it was a caterpillar. Instead of curing her of her
silly nerves however, it only seemed to make her worse,
and finally she used to take most of her tea or supper
away from the schoolroom and finish it in the privacy
of her bedroom. One day there were cucumber sandwiches, and Humpo, knowing this ahead (from Mipsie,
who always seemed to get inside information from the
footmen), laid his plans accordingly. When Mary had
retired to her room he got us to call her out on some
pretext, then slipping in he quickly substituted two sandwiches filled with young pale green newts, which really
looked extremely like sliced cucumber. Then when my
cousin returned and shut her door, we all crouched down
outside, and were soon rewarded by shriek after shriek
from Mary, while we stuffed our mouths with our hand-

[1] Lady Mary Twynge, now Countess Faggot.

kerchiefs to stifle our mirth. What guileless trifles do
cause amusement to the young!

Unlike Mipsie, I do not scorn tea as a meal, and before
the war I prided myself on my teas, especially on the
variety of my sandwiches, marmalade and mint, treacle
and curry powder, salmon paste and coffee essence
being some of my own favourite inventions. I liked to
ask a few congenial neighbours in to tea, and watch their
faces of surprise as they took the first bite. 'It's my own
idea. Do you like it?' I would ask. 'Yes, Lady Addle,
thank you,' or 'They are *very* original, Lady Addle,'
was the invariable answer, so I would know they must
have given pleasure to others besides myself.

Our menus are naturally restricted nowadays, but a
lot can still be done to make tea an outstanding meal,
as the following hints will show.

Cakes. To combat the fruit shortage, try using rose
hips, dried sloes or elder berries instead. They are a
little hard to bite, but remember what Mr. Gladstone
said about that in whichever year he said it.

For those who love seed cake and cannot obtain carro-
ways, bird seed or even grass seed (only the best variety,
such as would be used for a croquet lawn) are useful
substitutes.

A word to the wise. If you want to make Soda Cake,
or Soda Bread, be careful to use bi-carbonate of soda
and not the washing variety. It is a very easy mistake
to make—I did it myself—but it quite spoils the flavour.

Fancy things are less easy to achieve, but I have
managed Glucose brandy snaps (using liquid glucose of
course), blancmange eclairs stuffed with packet shape
instead of cream) and shrimp roll, which is of course
nothing but swiss roll made from a bought sponge
mixture, filled with shrimp paste to save jam, so no one
can say I am not venturesome.

Lastly there are still scones, oatcakes, girdle cakes, etc., to be made, and how delicious these simple things are. I have a special fondness for all Scottish bakery myself, as befitting the wife of a highland laird, and knowing how dear everything from Bonnie Scotland is to Addle too, I thought I would give him a surprise of some girdle cakes for tea. I have no girdle (one of our little evacuees naughtily threw it in the pond after I had specially cooked him some oatmeal biscuits for his birthday) but I improvised one from one of Addle's curling stones, which gave the cooking an extra Scotch connection somehow. I was a trifle nervous of telling my husband this, as he used to treasure the curling stones greatly, and always polished them on Sundays before the war. So I said nothing until he had helped himself to a girdle cake. Then I asked:

'What do you think I call these cakes?'

'Alfred the Great Cakes, I should think, my dear,' Addle said. (He had picked rather a black one.)

'No,' I answered triumphantly. 'I call them Curling cakes,' and then told him the reason. For one moment I thought he was upset, but he only rose and rang the bell.

'Crumpet's forgotten the whisky to-day,' he said.

'My dear boy,' I remonstrated. 'Whisky at tea-time!'

Never shall I forget his answer.

'Only to celebrate, my dear,' he replied. 'To celebrate your new girdle.'

And then people say that husbands are unsympathetic about housekeeping!

FROM GODIVA, COUNTESS COOT'S COOKERY BOOK, 1724

Halloween Cake. Into a bowl of fine copper admix two pounds of rank butter with the like body of coarse black sugar. Beat them into a rich cream with a brush of finest badger's hair. Put thereto a pounder of shredded tobacco leaf, new-landed from Bristol, and a proper pinch of snuff. Humify with olde port and bake very slow, so that ye cake when done be very heavy.

If a young maid is curious to know her fate in marriage, let her but wrap this cake in a snatch of old flannel, holding it in her arms and lying supine all the night long, and sure she will dream of her future husband. If she worsen thereafter, a phial of cuckoo-flower water will quickly revive her, though some say that agrimony hath the greater virtue.

XXI

MIPSIE RECALLS

(1) *Dinners*

I KNOW you will all be delighted to hear that I have persuaded Mipsie to take on the reminiscences of dinners, banquets and suppers, as I feel her experience has been fuller and perhaps more romantic than mine. Here goes then:

Dinner has always seemed to me to be the high spot of the day. How my spirits rise at the mere preparations for it! Sitting at my dressing-table clasping on three or four diamond bracelets perhaps, or putting the final touches to encourage the natural bloom of a rosy cheek. (I am lucky that I scarcely ever need make-up—only a few simple preparations of my own, on sale anywhere, £5 purchasing the whole outfit, including a wonderful eyelash grower that never runs, but is easily removed with a little neat brandy.) Meanwhile, my maid slides on a gossamer stocking, and my mind slides ahead. . . . What will the evening bring forth? What shall I gain— or what lesson shall I learn? For passionately as I love pleasure and excitement and vivid Life, I have never lost sight of the fact that we are in the world to make progress, to become richer by experience. . . .

Never has this been more true for me than in the days, just after the last war, when I was living in America. My husband at that time was Julius Block—and a more generous man never drew dividends. Every evening, when he came home from his office, he would bring me some little trifle—a tiara or a fox cape perhaps. Sometimes it was just a cheque. But even a piece of paper from him meant much to me. I remember one evening when he brought me only a beautiful spray of blood-red orchids. 'What lovely designs nature creates,' I exclaimed. 'How wonderful that spray would look carried out in rubies!' Next week he laid the ruby spray—an exact replica of the original—in my lap. Small wonder that later on—shortly before his financial crash and tragic death at his own revolver—when he failed often to bring me these nocturnal evidences of his affection, I felt it so deeply that I could not bring myself to dine with him. I would retire to my room and order a snack of caviare and game to be brought me in bed. Sad dinners those were for me—so sad that the shape of my champagne glass would often be dimmed by tears. . . .

But there were gay evenings too, especially in the early days, when we entertained on a large scale. America has always been a great country for stunts, and as I have a particularly fertile imagination my feature parties quickly became all the rage. There was my Borgia dinner, in which everyone had to bring a poor relation as a taster, my lagoon party, with pools of different rare wines, surrounded by oysters, all over the garden, and a nymph and satyr party, in which every man had to wear goat skins on his legs, and all the women were clad entirely in rose-petals. It took ten of my servants two whole days sweeping up the petals afterwards.

But the most amusing dinner of all was my pets' party, to which every guest brought their favourite animal or bird, who had their own meal served to them next door to their owner. This meant a good deal of preparation, as of course I didn't know exactly what to expect. One friend had threatened to bring a leopard. That meant having raw meat ready to hand. Then fish for cats (dover soles) bird seed and dog biscuits in plenty had to be laid in. I ordered a hundredweight of buns in case of elephants; dozens of beautiful presents as favours too. Every dog and cat had a collar studded with solid gold, with my initials on it, every bird a jewelled cage. When my guests were leaving, however, I saw to my horror that Mrs. Dwight B. Swatt, wife of the insecticide million-aire, was leaving with her pet—a delightful monkey in a tail coat—bearing no gift. 'My dear,' I said to her. 'How awful! Where is your pet's favour?' 'It's all right, Mipsie lamb,' she replied. 'I've got my little white mouse, with your gorgeous little platinum tread-wheel, in my reticule. This isn't a pet. It's my husband.' It was quite true. It was Dwight Swatt, whom no one had ever seen before, as he was too busy making fortunes.

Many other dinners I remember keenly, from big house-party affairs at Brisket Castle, where we would often have so many dukes staying with us that I would ena mena mina mo for which was to sit next to me at dinner, to homely little meals à deux at Foyot's or Larue. How often I would feel too that I had achieved more somehow in the simple environment of the latter, rather than from all the grandeur of the former. This was mainly Oxo's fault (my first husband) as he would tact-lessly bear down upon me after dinner, when I was just cementing the warm beginning of a friendship started under the mellowing influence of dinner, with some silly suggestion of bridge or billiards. The golden thread would be snapped—the contact broken—and per-haps a firm friend and supporter, all too sorely needed by those of us who happen to be blessed (or should I say cursed?) with beauty, lost for ever.

Lasting friendship. Is it so much to ask? Someone whose solid, unwavering support will stand the test of time and importunity. Yet husbands get divorced or die, bachelors marry, old friends lose their worth, even millionaires go bankrupt or make cruel wills, as I know to my cost, having married three. And so life goes on . . . just—as the poet says—one darned husband after another.

(2) *Banquets and Suppers*

Blanche wants me to write about banquets, but though I suppose no woman in Europe has had a wider experience of these than myself, I cannot contemplate my memories without some bitterness of heart, when I think of the miseries I suffered from official banquets at Ekaterinbog, during the time when I was married to my third husband, Prince Fedor Ubetzkoi. Oh, the agony of mind and spirit at the long tedious affairs, the food—except the caviare, which was wonderful, being in every colour, blue, green, red, white, gold, as well as black—being so unpalatable to me that I would make a pretence of toying with eight or ten courses and leave the rest. Then the strange, barbarous customs emphasized my utter loneliness. It is considered, for instance, most ill-bred to pay court to wives in Ekaterinbog—only the unmarried women receive attention—so that I would have to sit by and watch Irina, my plain, hateful step-daughter, loaded with flowers and compliments, while I was treated as only a paid companion or an ex-Lord Mayor's wife would have been treated in my father's house.

Then the endless formalities depressed me, for I have ever loved simplicity and freedom, and my only joy was to escape it all, plead illness, and have dinner served to me quite alone—except for Mich (Fedor's brilliant and handsome twenty-five-year-old son, Prince Michel), in my little silver and blue boudoir which I christened

'Love-in-a-mist'.[1] I always call my pet rooms after flowers. . . . How these dinners—when they became known about—shocked the stiff court set! Almost as much as when Mich and I tarred and feathered an Archimandrite! But we were always up to some pranks. . . . Yet the only time when Irina, in her jealous fury, burst into our sanctuary, all she found was Mich and me sitting on a couch in front of the fire, playing cat's cradle with my petticoat ribbons! But even then she dared to say things which cut me to my stepmother's heart, though I said nothing in return, judging gentleness to be the best answer to malice. In fact, from that day onwards, I never spoke to her again.

I have always adored childish games and fancies (I have introduced 'Sardines' into five Royal households— and what a success it has been too!), just as it is the child in me that loves the sparkle of diamonds . . . the faery gleam of platinum. This elfin streak in my character has often been misunderstood and sometimes got me into hot water, and I remember, in this connection, one special time when I was staying—before the last war—at the Imperial Court of Germany, which was even more formal than Ekaterinbog. There was a very rich and dashing man, Count von Saurkraut, who had a great reputation for sending little *billets-doux* to his lady friends. I thought it would be fun to see if this were true, so during a state banquet one night I wrote, by way of a non-committal opening, 'Are you the handsome Count von Saurkraut?' screwed the note into a ball, and had it slipped into one of his oysters instead of the real pearl which the Emperor, as a charming gesture, had ordered in every guest's plate. (I had the Count's

---

[1] Mipsie evidently inherits her love of this particular floweret from my mother, whose lovely poem on the subject I give at the end of this letter.

real pearl removed and brought to me to make the deception complete.) He replied, 'I am handsome only if you find me so.' The note was cunningly folded to look like one of the almond water-lilies in our *consommé*. I next scribbled 'Handsome is as handsome does'—and saw it deftly slid in between his foie gras and its aspic covering.

Then came a pause, while the Count kept looking towards me as though weighing something in his mind. At length came his answer nestling under the pastry lid of my *vol-au-vent*: 'Command me!' My heart leapt at the words. I replied in French: '*Je ne peux pas commander un inconnu,*' which message was neatly folded in an ortalan's wing. His answer, curled oh so tightly, into a fragment of spaghetti was 'Where can I see you alone?' I replied, giving him the whereabouts of my suite, but alas, the note, though beautifully disguised as a cream cone, never reached its destination. Unnoticed by both of us, the Count's wife, who was seated four places away from him on the same side (I was opposite), had observed the whole drama, and now when the tray of cream cones was handed to her, instead of taking the one intended for her, she reached beyond and helped herself to the sweet which should have been her husband's. With dilated eyes of horror I watched the Countess unfold and read my message—then, with one mocking triumphant look at me, she deliberately swallowed the note! I never saw either husband or wife—or, naturally, the note—again. As always, what was only innocent fun on my part was wilfully misconstrued by a jealous woman. These are the thorns which an English Rose— if she is beautiful—has to endure. . . .

Supper . . . How can I write of that delicious and romantic meal? On looking back in my diaries I find I have received 93 proposals during supper, nearly 50 per cent of them being for marriage. It can be readily understood therefore how hard I find it to speak of these precious moments, which must involve the names of the highest in the land. Yet memories haunt me . . . the gay suppers during a ball, the more serious ones which one would sit out. The brilliant supper-parties after the opera or the ballet, when my friends used to say they did not know which sparkled most, my jewels or my wit. Most dear of all, the private room suppers . . . shaded lights, special flowers, wonderful food and wines. Ah, those private rooms of yesteryear! What has befallen you now? Your *raison d'être* must surely be gone—for how can a man drink champagne out of the clumsy shoe of an A.T.S. officer? Or pin camellias on the serge bosom of a warden? Or wind pearls through the cropped hair of a land girl? And the aftermath of supper, what of that? The last tube home instead of the waiting limousine. Fifty common cigarettes instead of a jewelled cigarette-case. A few savings certificates instead of a block of oil shares. . . . These, to me, are the horrors of war.

Yours sincerely and beautifully,

MILLICENT BRISKETT.

I almost hesitate to print the following poem written by my mother while on her honeymoon, because it seems to lay bare some secret and terrible sorrow of which of course I know nothing. But after all, many of the great poets' finest creations unlocked the tragic secrets of their hearts, so I feel my dear mother will forgive me for including this, as some of her best work.

A BRIDE'S THOUGHTS

Love-in-a-mist,
Love-in-a-mist,
How sweet you were to me.
Shrouded and dim,
The thought of him
Was purest ecstasy.

He came one day
And stole away
My heart, when first he kissed
My finger tips—
But not my lips.
You were still Love-in-a-mist.

I stood beside
Him as a bride.
Was it but yesterday?
My bouquet fair,
With maiden hair,
What has become you to-day?

Love-in-a-mist,
Love-in-a-mist,
Oh, teach me to be brave.
My marriage vow
Will show me how
A countess should behave.
But Love, ah Love, I cry in vain,
Would you were in a mist again.

XXII

AL FRESCO

I FEEL almost as though I should apologize for writing this week's letter myself, after the wonderful treat we have been given of Mipsie's romantic and fascinating memoirs. Life for her has ever been full and rich and gay and vivid. She has dared all, never counting the cost—indeed, she has often said, with her enchanting, whimsical humour, that she has always left someone else to count the cost.

To-day I am going to write about picnics, because I look on them as so essential and delightful a part of our English life, that they cannot be omitted from any chronicle of meals.

I myself love a picnic of all things, and consider that food tastes twice as nice when eaten *al fresco*. My husband, unfortunately, feels quite the opposite. To begin with, he has a childish dislike—I would almost say fear if I didn't know him to be a soldier and a brave gentleman—of wasps. And though I have made for all my friends pretty and useful little brooches in the form of bunches of grapes, the fruit being made of tiny blue bags in case of bee stings, and the leaves of tinted lumps of soda for wasp stings, Addle utterly refuses to wear one and simply flaps *The Times* (which he insists on taking on a picnic, thereby, to my mind, completely ruining the idyllic spirit) at the wasps, which only seems to encourage them. 'Really, my dear boy,' I said to him once, 'you're behaving like a child of two.' 'I wish I were a child of two,' he replied. 'Then I wouldn't have been allowed to come at all.'

223

It is somewhat strange that I should still love picnics, for in my childhood these were often rather formal and alarming affairs—at any rate when my grandmother, the Duchess of Droitwich, was staying with us. She was exceedingly fastidious about everything—not only the scrupulous cleanliness of the spot we chose, but other things had to be considered; the sun, lest it should be too strong for her complexion, which was wonderful, like painted canvas; the wind, in case it should bring any unpleasant farmyard odours nigh. Then there had to be some trees or bushes near-by where the manservants could wait—unseen, yet ready to come immediately when summoned. On one occasion, I remember, the search for the perfect spot continued so long that eventually we arrived back at Coots Balder at four o'clock and ate our lunch on the terrace. My father was much more happy-go-lucky, in fact almost Bohemian, about picnics. He would never mind drinking his port out of a tumbler, and often took only one footman with us on the expedition.

Nowadays, who has time for picnics, I wonder? Old-time, romantic ones I mean. Of picnic food—snatched sandwiches in between war jobs—there is plenty. One friend of mine, Dame Winifred Paddock, boasts that she has had potted meat sandwiches for lunch every day for five years. I am glad to say she has just been given another decoration for her self-sacrificing work. Indeed, from the moment she rises at seven-thirty till she returns at eight o'clock to the dinner so beautifully cooked for her by her husband, Admiral Sir Horsa Paddock, her life is almost entirely spent in taking the chair. Sometimes she even takes it away with her from a meeting by mistake, so engrossed is she with the matter on hand. Last holidays, when her two boys came back from Harrow she did not know them; frequently she does not know

MY FATHER, THE 13TH EARL COOT

on which committee she is sitting till the end of the meeting (for she is chairman of twenty-eight and vice-chairman of seventeen). What man can produce a record like that, I ask?

But to return to picnices, I was quite forgetting our Institute ones, which are still going strong, especially hip and haw, nettle and salvage picnics. For the latter—always nearest my heart—we had a fag-end tea, just outside a camp near Bengers, and had picked up dozens of useful cigarette ends and cartons, when we were rather rudely banished by a sentry. There was also a very successful scrap metal outing in our woods, with an amusing sequel which I will relate.

We were just going home with a good, but not outstanding, collection of oddments, when one of our most energetic members came running up to me: 'Oh, Lady Addle, we have just found a splendid lot of galvanized iron bins. The others are bringing them along.' At that moment more members arrived carrying, to my dismay, several of the new pheasant feeders which Addle had proudly installed just before the war. However, I couldn't disappoint the members by telling them to replace them, and they were not in use now of course, so we put them on the handcart and took them back to Bengers. Of course the first person we met was Addle! His jaw dropped at sight of us, but before he could speak I cried gaily: 'Isn't it wonderful, dear? We've done so well for salvage! We're just going to weigh our lot at the stables, and the Council will call for them in the morning.' My husband said nothing, realizing from my words that the die was cast.

That night I slept badly—perhaps I was tired from the day's exertions, or perhaps I was a little worried about the pheasant feeders, though Addle had said no more and seemed quite cheerful all the evening. Anyway, in the middle of the night, I thought I would fetch my knitting and started downstairs. To my surprise, the light was on in the hall, and looking over the banisters I could see my husband and Crumpet, our butler, descending the last few stairs, carrying something between them. As I waited, breathless, I heard Addle say:

'We must get the weight exactly right or her Ladyship will find out. Don't forget, Crumpet, *she must never know*.'

I stole back to my room, my heart warm with loving gratitude to my dear husband, who, rather than distress me, was evidently sacrificing something of his own for salvage.

It wasn't till months afterwards that I found out that he had disposed of some japanned trunks I had in my trousseau—never used, I know, but of some sentimental value nevertheless. But I suppose one can't expect men to be sensitive about such things.

THE GARDEN FRONT

WRITING of such al fresco delights as picnics reminds me that as yet I have said nothing of our duty to our country on the Garden Front.

I think no family in Europe can ever have loved gardens as did we Coots, nor have been the happy possessors of more perfect examples of the horticulturalist's art. I remember walking one beautiful summer evening with the late Mr. Thomas Hardy along our armorial walk, in which every bed was shield-shaped, with coats of arms of various noble families related to ours worked out in flowers. I knew how the simple beauty of this would appeal to that great man so was not surprised when he walked almost the whole length of it in silence. Suddenly he stopped. 'Shall we turn back?' he asked. 'It is getting chilly and you have on a thin dress.' I understood his reserve. He did not trust himself to speak of what moved him deeply.

Other gardens I recollect with pleasure, and also with amusement. We used to stay sometimes with a connection of my mother's, the Duke and Duchess of Stayes, at Corset Castle (one of the old-time, impregnable keeps), which was famous for its topiary. The Duke, who was a bit of a character, was also an expert topiarist himself, and used to steal out in the early morning with his own tool and amuse himself in one of the long yew avenues. Sometimes, however, his rather erratic fancy would carry him too far and he would model something to which the Duchess—who had a very delicate mind—would take exception. The offending yew would then, by her orders, be covered up with a tarpaulin until the head gardener could clip it in to some more prudent shape. I well remember one day, whilst staying at Corset when we were still in our teens, coming on the Duchess at the entrance to one of the avenues. She was white to the lips and shaking like a leaf. 'You can't go down there, children,' she said to Mipsie and me. 'I have just sent for the tarpaulin.' Next morning, I woke early and missed Mipsie—she and I shared a room together. Soon she returned fully dressed. I asked her where she had been. 'The Duke took me under the tarpaulin,' she replied—but she would never tell me what she had found there.

The same Duke it was who insisted on being married in one of the beautiful suits of armour belonging to the Stayes family. He looked a magnificent sight, I am told —so magnificent that when the time came to leave for the honeymoon nothing would induce him to remove his armour (he was always rather a vain man, inheriting this quality I fancy from his French mother, who was a de la Brassière), and eventually he departed seated on the box of the carriage, since it was wellnigh impossible for him to get inside. Hardly a propitious start for a honeymoon! But far worse was to come. In the rush of departure the Duke unfortunately left behind the only valet who understood the intricacies of the armour suit so that he was quite unable to remove it at all until the man arrived the following morning. Meanwhile, the young Duchess, in a state of collapse, had returned to her mother, and it was some time before the breach was sufficiently healed for her to go back to her husband again. The marriage was never a happy one.

Another garden with delightful memories is that of the Princess of Splasche at Schloss Morgenbad. Born a simple English Royalty, Pansy Splasche could not bear the formality of the German Court life, where it was *de règle* for four flunkeys to precede her into every room in the palace, however private her reasons for entering it. The vast and stately gardens, in spite of their beauty, gave her a sense of oppression.   So, unbeknown to her husband she designed and had carried out in a secluded corner what she called her 'Garden of Destiny'.   It was planted in the English haphazard way, yet with a meaning.   For every crowned head was represented by a shrub, titled friends by flowers, and less well-born people by vegetables. Some of my happiest memories are of staying at Morgenbad when I first married, and the fun Pansy and I had arranging the garden; pricking out a leek for the charming young English tutor who had just arrived, and then finding out that he was heir to a baronetcy and having to change the leek for a delphinium; removing the white lilies she always planted for every débutante and changed for pink or orange one when they married (but Mipsie was always a tiger lily for some reason or other).   Yet at the same time the garden must have had its sad side, when the crowned heads of Europe began to disappear.   I was with Pansy when she pulled up the Empress Eugénie (a fine Magnolia) and shall never forget how she wept.   Now I believe the Garden of Destiny is a potato patch, which seems somehow symbolic of Life in this sadly socialist age.

But indeed, the same might be said of many of our lovely English gardens; only the exquisite emerald lawns and brilliant flower-beds have given their services for England, which dignifies their sad state.   The beautiful clock golf course at Coot's Balder (except for one corner of it, the sixth hole, which my brother Crainy, who was a first-class athlete, once did in two, so the strip is railed off in commemoration of his feat) is now given over to groundsel for the estate canaries, the Duke of Quorn's fernery is a beetery, while Lord Sealyham's famous eighteenth century maze was sacrificed to make asparagus beds for his evacuees; an extremely difficult task, involving endless labour digging the beds in all the tortuous twists and turns of the maze. The sad thing is that the labour was in vain, as it transpired afterwards that the evacuees would only eat asparagus if it had first been tinned. However, the family used up the genuine article, so for once virtue was rewarded.

As for our garden at Bengers, we have of course tried to do our bit for the garden front, but I fear that it has not been altogether successful. I sacrificed my water garden to aubergines, only to find that they would not grow in a damp place, or in fact in England at all. I installed tomato plants in the weeping willow walk, thinking their gay colour would light up the avenue, which gets practically no sun during the day (nor at night of course), but the tiresome things just would *not* ripen. I also tried, unsuccessfully, to grow mustard and cress, on old pieces of Addle's shirts, on the statuary along the terrace. Then we have been very unfortunate with pests. All our radishes have suffered from slut weevil, and an entire crop of early parsley was devoured by the fell sod fly. In fact, so ill-fated did we appear to be in this direction, that at one time I thought it might be best to yield to Dame Nature's stern decrees, and so made all plans for encouraging the woolly aphis in our orchards, as I felt sure there must be some method of gathering and spinning their product in order to save shipping space for imported wool. I am convinced that there was something in the idea, but sad to say Addle put his foot down and absolutely refused to allow it. He seemed to think it would be bad for the trees in some way.

XXIV

MANNERS MAKYTH MAN

PERHAPS this chapter should have been penned earlier, for I am going to write on manners, which are indeed the alpha of social and family life, and in these democratic days are permitted to all. When I was young, 'good manners' was a phrase only employed in our own set. The lower orders had to show respect, the middle classes merely to keep in the background. Nowadays, though, the butcher, the baker and the candlestick maker are all encouraged to be gracious. I am sure my father would have turned in his grave if he had been alive.

My old home, Coots Balder, was noted for exquisite manners. I can see my mother now, seated at tea on the terrace when several visitors were arriving. She would often rise from her seat to greet them, and would invariably shake hands, whatever their rank. Perhaps some young guest would be shy. Then would shine forth her innate charm and ease of manner. Immediately she would find some topic of conversation which held a mutual interest, such as the weather. 'I do hope the rain is going to keep off,' perhaps she would say. The visitor would then eagerly respond that he or she hoped so too. Enthusiasm would banish shyness, and the conversational ball would be set rolling.

Mipsie tells me how grateful she has often been to Mama for this early training. To this day, when meeting a stranger, she at once mentions the Ritz in Paris. If it strikes a chord, well and good, if not she moves on to another guest.

I think the most perfect example of good manners I

231

have ever known was during a dinner-party at Coots Balder, when dear old Lord Hangover, who had all the courtliness of a real knight-errant, was staying with us. He was sitting next to a very stout lady, and when she bent forward to talk to him her dainty lace handkerchief fell out of the folds of her fichu into his ice cream. Rather than embarrass her by drawing attention to the mischance he *ate every scrap* of the handkerchief without any signs of distaste whatever. Ah, those dinner-parties in the good old days—what dignity and wisdom pervaded the table talk. And if conversation languished, there were always little jokes like plate lifters—small rubber bulbs attached to tubing which went under the table-cloth and suddenly lifted up your neighbour's plate—to keep the table in a roar. False noses, sham ink blots, etc.— those were brilliant days indeed.

Yet the art of conversation is needed more than ever now, when attention is often best diverted from the food. I have become quite an adept at this, and if I am particularly doubtful about a dish I often start to relate some anecdote during the previous course, timing it so that the dénouement comes at the exact moment when I wish everyone's mind drawn from what they are eating. Sometimes however this little ruse miscarries, as happened the other day.

I had had rather an unlucky time with a cake which I had made the week before from mangel-wurzel flour. (I thought if flour can be made from potatoes and soya beans one could grind it out of roots, and so one can, only unfortunately it tastes rather strong and also makes the cake decidedly heavy and hard.) However, one must not waste food in war-time so, after my cake had remained practically untouched for days, I boiled it up as a pudding (having soaked it in a little liquid paraffin to soften it first), then covered it with my strongest sauce—chocolate, vanilla and ginger. And I told one of my best stories—of how my inimitable brother Humpo had once substituted quinine for Kummel for a whole dinner-party—timing it to last through two courses. But whether it was that the first course of eggs and bacon took rather longer to eat because I stupidly quite forgot to cook the bacon, or what, but my story was over before the pudding, and of course there was dead silence when the plates were handed, in the middle of which Addle—who was un-expectedly present—struck the pudding with his spoon with a resounding blow that echoed through the room. At the same time one of our little evacuees whispered loudly: 'Mum, it's the rock of Gibraltar again!' It was a somewhat awkward moment saved, I congratulate myself, by the art of conversation. 'Yes, Gary dear,' I said. 'And that rock belongs to Britain, so Britons mustn't shrink from it'—and Britons they proved them-selves, every one of them!

Of course there are other facets of good table manners, such as eating, what one does with one's hands, and so on. Shyness often leads people to do extraordinary things. I had a friend, whose name I had better not mention, who was ostracized from Society because of a strange habit of modelling sheep with her crumbled bread. The shyer she was, the larger were the sheep. Eventually she was cured in a home, I believe, by being given only toast, but it was too late to regain the high social place to which she was born.

I always advise débutantes for their first season to avoid anything which needs skill in handling, like limp asparagus, or tricky bones. I shall never forget Margaret, when she was about fourteen, tackling a poussin at lunch; her knife slipped, and the wish bone struck an Eastern potentate full between the eyes! It was particularly unfortunate, as it transpired that in his country to strike a man on the forehead with a wish bone constituted some special insult to his mother, so the august personage immediately left Bengers in high dudgeon!

Nowadays I am told people pick up all manner of things at cocktail parties (to which I have never been!) and eat them with their fingers. Not only biscuits and light sandwiches either, but actually more substantial food, such as sausages. It seems a strange time to eat what amounts to a meal, but Mipsie tells me there were, before the war, many delightful young men in Mayfair whose sole subsistence was these precarious repasts, so of course it was really a kind of philanthropy—a modern equivalent of slumming perhaps? As I say, times have changed indeed.

XXV

MAKE DO AND MEND

I THINK you may be interested to hear something about our Make Do and Mend Club in Great Bengers, of which I am proud to be president, though the moving spirits are two of our oldest and most energetic residents, Miss Rinse and Miss Snodgrass, and a wonderful job they have done, especially when one considers that they haven't been on speaking terms for thirty years. (The breach occurred over a mending misunderstanding, oddly enough. A young curate of Great Bengers in 1913 rather deceitfully gave both girls his socks to mend, without telling either of the other's help. But every woman knows her own darns, and soon the whole wretched affair came to light, and a great scandal it caused. But time alone can heal these unhappy disputes.)

The club meets at the Village Hall every Monday, and the terms of membership are that everyone should be prepared to attend a meeting wearing at least three garments or accessories made from something else. I am *ex officio* on the committee of course, but I insisted on proving my worth by coming in a hydrangea mauve jumper made from a dyed roller towel, a smart pair of green gloves contrived from an old butler's apron, and a sunset-coloured necklace of ruddy plum stones. And they were kind enough to say that I sailed in with flying colours.

To the meetings come not only our own villagers but, I rejoice to say, many from surrounding villages as well, bringing their wardrobe and household troubles. We have a special advice table for what to do with holes, and a lovely piece bag, gay with coloured patches for pockets, appliqué flowers and fruit, etc. Often we darn dutch boy fashion and let the patch brighten as well as mend. One member proudly wears a worn knitted costume, every thin part darned over with the flags of all our Allies!

Then there is a cleaning hint table, and you wouldn't believe the strange stains we help to remove. Ink blots from biscuits, lipstick from cricket bats, port stains from bathing gowns, iron mould from shaving brushes and so on.

And talking of shaving, I was told a very good way of economizing in razor blades the other day. Rub your face—your husband's face that is—with kitchen salt overnight and put a saucer of water by his bedside. The hairs will grow twice as fast because they will stretch out thirstily for the water, and he will be able to cut off two days' growth with one shave—thus saving the use of his razor altogether the following day.

To return to our club, perhaps the most attractive section of all is the children's advice table, where school children's outfits are cut down for toddlers, toddlers' for tots, tots' for B.I.A. (babies in arms) and B.I.A. for their parents. Thus the whole family help each other. For instance, when big brother John leaves school, his discarded satchel makes splendid hardwearing crawlers for little Doris, whose outgrown pinny cuts into new bibs for baby Gordon. And the best bits of the old bibs, herringboned together, make a lovely face flannel for Daddy or perhaps a smart collar for mother.

Toys too. Everyone knows the kind of humpy bottle which has no use after the contents have been used. We cover these with material, sew on some jaunty feathers for a tail, add a painted cardboard head and legs, and there is the loveliest cockyolley-bird. The only thing against it is that being glass, it is rather dangerous for children to play with, but we are now trying to get a government permit for wood, to carve into the same shape.

We have lectures of course, to keep us up to the mark. Not only on Make do and Mend, but any household problems that might interest our members. 'Twenty things to do with father's trousers', 'Making the best of a bad egg,' 'What to do with Grannie when she's bed-ridden' and 'New homes for old earwigs' were a few recent ones.

Finally, the members and I are slowly compiling a book of a hundred home hints, culled from the experiences of all, which are really invaluable, and which Mr. Dalton will be very foolish if he does not accept for the Board of Trade when finished. I quote a page, chosen at random, to show how thoroughly we have covered our ground.

A cure for sleeplessness. Take a large Spanish onion to bed with you. You will have such a bad night that the following one you will find that nothing will keep you awake.

For those whose figure keeps on widening (like myself!) Cut one dress down the middle, embroider gay-coloured eyelet holes, then lace it with dyed string over another tighter dress of a contrasting shade.

A good substitute for sun tan is ammonia mixed with brown boot polish. Rub up with an old sock.

Badges. Military badges, scout and guide devices, or shields from your children's outgrown school blazers, make attractive *motifs* to cover holes or worn parts in underclothes.

A cure for bags under the eyes. Sleep upside down and the bags will often work through to a less noticeable part of the body.

Stockings that are hopelessly gone at the foot make excellent winter coats for dachshunds.

Never throw away corset bones. They make into bookmarkers, poker chips, spaghetti winders, toothpicks for horses.

A good tooth paste for children is scouring powder mixed with chocolate malt spread. They won't shirk teeth cleaning then!

Hysteria in piano tuners is easily cured by laying the man on the keyboard and opening his instrument case.

Brighten up old buns by wrapping them in used flypapers and leaving in the sun for half an hour. They will be as shiny as the pre-war article—and a few flies will be all to the good, giving the illusion of plentiful currants.

When you are washing dainty lingerie do not include in the same basin any golf balls, doormats, fountain pens, bicycle baskets, or any Benares brass article.

To preserve the life of a housemaid—if you are fortunate enough to have one—warm slightly before use.

XXVI

THE GREAT ADVENTURE

EVER since I wrote in these pages a week or so ago that I had never been to a cocktail party, I have been besieged by letters from friends, both known and unknown, telling me that it is an experience which I should not miss. Even Boadicea Broadmoor,[1] whom I have known since childhood—our fathers are on the same page of Whittaker together which seems to make a special bond between us—who I thought had never touched anything but Imperial Tokay with soda water all her life, wrote to me that she had given a cocktail party (for the coming of age of her grandson,[2] 'Boy' Borstal) in the housekeeper's room of their Dorset home which is all that is left to them by the Ministry of Economical Relations—I *think* I have the name right—who have taken over the house.

Boadie said it was a highly successful party, enjoyed by all except possibly the Duke, who unfortunately had his ear trumpet filled up with whisky by a young American officer, in error. And she seemed to think I was rather behind the times for not giving one too. I don't feel this comes very well from Boadie, who was born in '68, whereas I was born in the summer of '69 so am considerably her junior. However, it put me on my mettle and I was determined to try.

But how to accomplish it? Bengers has no divans, no tiger-skin rugs or long cigarette holders, and I certainly have no trousers, even if Addle would consent to my wearing them, which I greatly doubt. Yet I had always

[1] The Duchess of Broadmoor.
[2] Viscount Borstal.

understood that these things were inseparable from cocktail parties. True, I rather dreaded being seen by the county lying on a divan in trousers and smoking a cigarette for the first time, but I thought if Boadie Broadmoor could do it I would not shrink, if only I could obtain the accessories.

I was just contemplating ringing up Harfridge's hire department when Mipsie came into the room, and thankfully I remembered that she always knows about everything. She immediately took a weight off my mind by telling me that cocktail parties were not quite as I imagined, that divans, tiger-skin rugs and trousers are quite unnecessary, and in fact, the only difficulty nowadays is in the materials for the cocktails themselves. But if I would give her *carte blanche* she would obtain them somehow and manage the whole thing, even down to mixing the drinks herself. The only thing was, she would have to have a new dress as none of her present ones were suitable (for some technical reason no doubt which is beyond my ignorance), but I gladly wrote her out a cheque for £75 which she said would just cover the ingredients for the party and the dress she had in mind.

Meanwhile, I sent out the invitations. They included several people on whom I have not called, such as the Brawns at the Grange, who made their money in linseed and are anything but aristocratic, and the Dibble-Smiths —a rather unpopular couple who have never been known to discuss anyone else in the neighbourhood, so it is thought there must be some mystery about them— and a very odd pair of girls at Little Bengers Cottage, who breed borzois and both wear Russian cavalry uniform. Then I thought it would be kind to ask poor dull Mr. Knoop, who lives such a sad life always writing about prehistoric bangles, and Mrs. Tansy and her terribly plain Christabel, and of course Miss Rinse and

THE PRINCESS PANSY OF SPLASCHE

Miss Snodgrass, though it is well known that they hate attending any social function where they might have to speak to each other.

The day of the party arrived. I felt rather nervous, especially as Addle said he *must* cut down some big nettles in the grove, and therefore couldn't appear. But Mipsie, who is always so sympathetic and understanding, brought me something in a glass which she said would buck me up—and indeed it did, besides being delicious. I went downstairs feeling ready for anything.

And oddly enough, that feeling continued all the afternoon. With a glass of this same delightful concoction of Mipsie's in my hand I found myself laughing as I hadn't laughed since I was a schoolgirl at Mr. Knoop's jokes—I had no idea he was so witty or that prehistoric bangles were such fascinating things. Everyone in fact seemed to be so entertaining, the Brawns far less vulgar that I thought, or anyway so good-hearted and nice withal that one couldn't object, and to my surprise I found myself promising to go to tea with them to see their calceolarias. The Dibble-Smiths too were most pleasant, and I came to the conclusion that they had been much maligned, for towards the end of the party I heard them discussing everyone in Great Bengers quite loudly—just like ordinary people—with Christabel Tansy, who was looking really charming, positively pretty I thought. I was a little horrified to see the girls from Little Bengers arriving in their cavalry uniforms, with three enormous borzois, but I decided after a time that it was rather narrow-minded of me, and that they looked as splendid as their dogs. To my surprise one of the girls arrived this morning with a borzoi puppy which she assures me I ordered at the party, though I can't help thinking it is her misunderstanding, as I have no recollection of it. However, it is a dear puppy, and will be most useful for eating up things I make mistakes over, such as burnt cakes, etc.

Best of all though was the wonderful reconciliation between Miss Rinse and Miss Snodgrass, who actually walked out of the room arm in arm! I hear they are not speaking again to-day, but Mipsie suggests that another cocktail party might heal the breach permanently, and really I feel that I wouldn't mind repeating such an enjoyable afternoon, even though I can't deny that I found it decidedly tiring. I had rather a bad headache next day, quite natural, Mipsie says, and due I suppose to the somewhat overwhelming buzz of conversation to a quiet country dweller like myself.

But at any rate Boadie Broadmoor can't say I am behind the times now.

The foregoing chapter reminds me of another friend, who has suffered deeply—Mena, Viscountess Artery and Blood, who had been forced, at long last, to leave Vein House. I wrote this little poem to commemorate her fortitude in disaster.

A WOMAN'S MARTYRDOM

She dwelt within a mansion fair,
Fit lodging for a king.
Full seventy bedrooms were to spare,
Not counting the servants' wing.
Old masters hung upon the walls,
And pearls upon her breast.
And many and famous were the balls
Enjoyed at her behest.

The first war came—her income crashed,
While her commitments grew.
Her life's brief happiness was smashed.
By Death—its Duties too.
Super-tax mounted; then this war
The final outrage made.
Her cultured home was commandeered
By the earth-bound Board of Trade.

She dwelleth in a garret now,
Full seven stories high.
She buys her simple needs herself
To make the days go by.
Alone—save for three faithful maids,

Her splendid Rolls no more;
So, shopping done, a humble taxi
Takes her to her door.

Wearily she ascends by lift,
Enters her flat again,
And dazedly, like one adrift
She gazes down Park Lane.
Her white, emaciated hands
Play with her diamond rings,
And her white soul knows the agony
That destitution brings.

XXVII

A POT POURRI OF CONSERVES

It is so wonderful to know that I have been able to help my Public with these cookery crumbs from my table, and it gives me real pleasure when they write and tell me so. 'Experimenting with your recipes has enriched our silo no end,' writes a plumber from Essex, and though I am not sure in exactly what way this was achieved, I rejoice to think I have helped him and his worthy family. Plumbers do a fine job, I think; always stopping leakages and making things flow more easily. If we could all do that in life, how much happier the world would be.

But I must get to this week's subject, which is jams, jellies and pickles. Perhaps I am specially qualified to write of these, for my old home, Coots Balder, was famous for all of them. I remember one cook, Mrs. Cramp, who always produced the most beautiful glowing colours with her jams. We never knew her secret, which was closely guarded, until one day, when some greengage jam was in the making, my mother discovered her in the drawing-room in the act of snipping an olive green chenille ball off a curtain. It then transpired that she had for years included in her preserves small pieces of stuff of specially rich colour—a bit of crimson brocade here, an inch of blackberry coloured gimp there—all cut with such consummate skill that it was impossible to detect the theft. 'Ah, my lady,' Mrs. Cramp said when Mama remonstrated with her, 'there's nothing that makes a good jam like a piece of material from a good house.' My mother saw the force of this argument, and Mrs. Cramp was allowed to continue her snipping undeterred.

Not only could we boast of our colours but also of our variety. Nowadays people seem too apprehensive about wasting sugar to experiment, and hence some splendid ingredients wither in the fields and hedgerows for want of plucking. The common burr for instance, soaked overnight and well stewed, makes an unusual jelly with a sweetish taste not unlike plate powder. Acorns, boiled to a pulp, will help to eke out your quinces if they are scarce. Then potato jam, with a little cochineal and some very fine grass seed for pips, with a raspberry jam label on the jar, does splendidly for people who have, either temporarily or permanently, lost their taste. I find my evacuees always demand raspberry or strawberry jam, so I have been reduced to innocent little ruses such as I quote above, or sometimes to boiling up a pound jar of one of them with a pint of conker stock, which sets into two or three jars of a kind of jelly-ish jam, or perhaps more accurately, a jam-ish jelly.

I must stress the importance of your jelly cloth. Most cookery books recommend flannel for straining. I go further and say that old flannel is the best, especially some personal belonging such as an old flannel hot-water bottle cover or a beloved dog's blanket, which seems in some strange way to give the jelly a very poignant flavour.

Now for pickles and chutneys. How well I remember the fascinating variety that used to be handed round at home. Puff balls in peach brandy, Indian swamp chutney, pickled limpets—recipes guarded with the cook's life, who would sometimes however refuse even to pass it on to her mistress. As in the case of old Lady Umbrage who gave her cook a silk dress, a canary in a cage and her fare from Norfolk to see the Crystal Palace, in order to coax from her the secret of her wonderful Egyptian pickle which she had learnt from being in service with Prince Waft el Rumfellah. When this failed, Lady Umbrage very reluctantly lowered her wages, locked her in the still room for twenty-four hours, and finally dismissed her without a character. Even so, the stubborn old woman refused to give up her recipe, which died with her.

But the story does not end there. My mother used to say that when Connie Umbrage put her hand to the plough she made hay while the sun shone, and she was now determined, as she had failed to wrest the secret from her cook in life, that she would obtain it by other means. It was in the early days of psychical research and there was a famous medium, Madame Bacteria, who was much patronized by Society at the time. She was supposed to be controlled by Cleopatra's asp and she always slept with two mummies on her bed. What more likely person, Lady Umbrage argued, for getting an Egyptian recipe either from the cook, or from Prince Rumfellah, also deceased? Mipsie, who is always so ready to help anyone in trouble, promised to arrange the whole thing beforehand, as Lady Umbrage was a little nervous of the strange atmosphere of a séance. Accordingly they arrived, and almost immediately, I gather, Cleopatra's asp came through, and introduced Prince Rumfellah. He said that that cook still flatly refused to pass on the secret but he would do so himself if Lady Umbrage would first take off all her rings and pass them to the person on her left— who happened to be Mipsie—as an expiation of her treatment of the cook. This done, he proceeded to give the recipe, which was an exceedingly complicated one, involving sending to the Sahara for a special kind of cactus. However, Lady Umbrage obeyed the instructions to the letter, though they cost her endless trouble and expense. The curious thing is that the pickle, when made, did not taste in the least like the original. The mystery has never been explained, but I think myself that the whole episode was probably intended as a lesson to Lady Umbrage not to dabble in the occult.

XXVIII

A DARK CLOUD

AN appalling tragedy has just descended upon our family, of which I hardly dare write, yet something stronger than me compels me to tell the truth, however bitter. My dear sister Mipsie has been arrested for dealings with the black market!

What my feelings are as I pen these words may well be imagined! Our family have always been *sans peur et sans reproche*—or at any rate from this kind of scandal. It is true the 7th Earl Coot, in 1784, was imprisoned for throttling a valet, and Lady Idina Coot, in 1820, was heavily fined for selling one of her children to pay a gambling debt, but these were mistakes at least in keeping with the dignity of the aristocracy, and not therefore the stain on the family honour that a charge of this kind presents. Poor darling, impetuous, generous Mipsie. Even her ex-husbands must surely weep for her now—the ones still alive, of course, I mean.

Because I need hardly say that it is that very impetuosity and generosity that has betrayed her. She herself is incapable of a dishonourable action—but I will tell the whole story.

It will be remembered that I mentioned in these pages some time ago a Firewatchers' Dance Club in which Mipsie was interested. I did not know then that she herself was the promoter and organizer of the whole thing. It was just another one of her brilliant conceptions born of an ardent desire to help humanity. The dance club was not for those who were actually firewatching—Mipsie would be the last person to distract men from their duty to king and country—but for those who *said they were firewatching*, and in reality sought a little sorely needed relaxation and change from the routine of home life. Yet with that capacity for detail which is said to be the hall-mark of genius, she saw to it that the room contained sufficient evidence of the members being on firewatch to satisfy anyone who was suspicious enough to intrude. Thus, round the walls stood water containers, with tin hats in artistically arranged groups hung above them. In between these were sand buckets, stirrup pumps and fire shovels. There was even a real fire engine which was converted into a bar. Mipsie was never entirely happy about this latter object, as she was unfortunately never able to obtain a licence for the club, which was in the cellar of a blitzed warehouse in Mayfair, by the way. Conscientious to a fault, she wished no slur, no smallest taint of dishonour to fall upon her club and its members, so she arranged for the fire engine quickly to be turned over to the distribution of tea and coffee only in the event of occasional visits from members' wives or the police.

Of course she sought the best of everything for her war-working menfolk. What woman worthy of the name would not? So when people offered her butter and eggs and sugar and hams, she very naturally accepted them, never grudging the price she had to pay for them. How should she—a duchess, chatelaine of Briskett Castle, hostess of a thousand parties in New York and Newport—how should she be able to think in the small mundane terms of rations and food points? Her soul was too big.

It was the same with clothes. She made a point of being at The Alert, as the club was called, as many nights as possible—no lazy deputizing for Mipsie—and naturally she would not wish to let her dear members down, for loyalty is the very core of her being, by appearing too often in the same dress. Friends offered to procure her

new ones without coupons. Trustingly she agreed.
Reckless and foolish she may have been—she was always
adorably heedless of practical matters—but who shall
blame her for the very impetuosity and wide-eyed confidence in the good faith of her friends that has always
been part of her innate charm.

The end came, as so often in poor Mipsie's career,
through the enmity of a woman. A guest member in
the A.R.P. had presented Mipsie with a brooch commemorating his war service, in the form of 'Heavy Rescue' in
brilliants. Unfortunately his wife, who had become
suspicious of her husband's frequent absence from home
in the evenings, traced him to The Alert, where the first
person she saw was Mipsie, wearing the brooch.
Immediately she declared that the whole idea of having
'Heavy Rescue' in diamonds had been hers, that her
husband had promised to have it made for her for her
birthday, and that Mipsie must have got the jewel instead
by some means more foul than fair. High words followed,
and the wife left the club that night a bitter, revengeful
enemy of my poor sister.

After that matters moved with a terrible and fatal
swiftness. Mipsie, fearing trouble, immediately dis-
mantled the bar and declared the club closed for two
nights. But before she could take any more precautions
the police were in The Alert, making a fuller investigation
than on any previous visit.

Alas, they found only too much. In the tin hats on
the walls were stocks of butter and eggs, the hollow shaft
of every shovel was filled with sugar, a ham lay hidden
in each false-bottomed sand bucket. As for the stirrup
pumps they were all laid on to beer barrels, while every
water container was discovered to be filled to the brim
with gin. (Half a guinea had been charged for lifting
the lid, to members—one guinea to non-members).

People of course always think the worst in this harsh world. Mipsie was not even allowed bail.

I have just been to see her in prison. She is shaken, but wonderfully calm and resigned. Indeed, her gratitude for even small things brought tears to one's eyes. The Chaplain was lending her his hot water bottle and the Prison Governor had just been to see her, she told me, to find out if she had everything she wanted. Shortly afterwards a frugal but not unpalatable meal of steamed sole and melon had been brought her. She described prison life as 'simple, but everything of the very best'.

XXIX

THE SILVER LINING

How true it is what the philosophers and wise men of old used to say, that every cloud has a silver lining. Ever since that sad time when Margaret's friendship with the Polish officer came to naught, I have rather dreaded—though it seems disloyalty to dear Mipsie even to think it—asking any other man to the house to meet my daughter (and it seemed too much to hope that she should find one herself *twice*), in case the same disaster should happen again. Mipsie does not realize the strength of her own charm, and I have often thought, when I have seen her drawing away—unconsciously no doubt—some young man from the girl he had previously appeared attached to, that there was little hope of a suitable marriage, or indeed any marriage at all, for Margaret while my beautiful sister lived at Bengers.

My first feeling then, when I opened my daughter's wonderful letter actually telling me of her *engagement*, was—though I hate to confess it—one of relief that Mipsie was safely under lock and key, even though the terrible circumstances of her arrest still appal me. Next moment, when I read that Margaret's fiancé was a Private Paul White, of the West Indian Regiment, the letter dropped from my nerveless hands. The West Indies—surely that must mean negroes. My daughter was going to marry a black man!

Every mother will feel for me. I had never expected anything for Margaret but, at the best, a new peer or a reasonably good younger son perhaps—at the worst, a gentleman farmer or plain business man. But this was something I had never contemplated in my wildest nightmares. And what would Addle say? How should I break it to him that his only daughter was going to cut herself off from civilization, and perhaps live in a wigwam and do native dances with feathers in her hair? (And Margaret's figure is far from its best when dancing too.)

But I have never shirked any task yet, and soon I was in Addle's study with the fatal letter. To my infinite relief he told me at once that I was under a misconception as to the West Indies, and that Mr. White was probably as fair as his name, and a British subject. My husband seemed far more concerned with his army rank than his complexion. 'Surely, my dear, you can soon put that right?' I said, and suggested that he should get Mr. White at least a Lieutenancy in the Guards. But to my surprise Addle told me it was quite impossible, even the War Office, apparently, having mixed themselves up with socialism nowadays, which seems sad indeed.

However, Mr. White arrived next day with Margaret and seemed delightful. Quite nice looking, with a high complexion that matches hers almost exactly and is a great bond between them, and pleasant though very quiet manners. He appeared devoted to Margaret, and never tired of gazing, indeed almost peering, at her. This was explained later by his admitting to extreme short sight, so that he is, even in his strongest spectacles, he told me, quite unable to make out the features of any face at all. Specialists have said that his sight may improve when he is forty, but I am not going to worry about that now. He will have married Margaret by then, and will have found out, I feel sure, what a dear girl she is in spite of everything. But indeed, she looked so radiant with happiness that I was hardly apprehensive about the actual wedding. All the same, I advised her to have only poor plain Christabel Tansy as bridesmaid, just to be on the safe side.

Paul White's people, we found, were coffee planters—quite well to do, though not, of course, of the social status that we should expect for our daughter. But her children will be half McClutch, quarter Coot, eighth Twynge—blue enough blood, surely, to permit of a little dilution. Besides, these are democratic days, and *noblesse* must *oblige*, even in marriage.

And so the great day drew near. I sacrificed all Addle's coupons for a wedding-dress for my dear girl—since she seemed disappointed at the idea of having one made of the splinter proof net which we have just peeled off the windows at Bengers—and I sent off the invitations on real pre-war cards, as I was lucky enough to buy up a stock of a deceased dentist's appointment cards, and used the other side. I even managed confetti, by getting round the superintendent of a bus depot near here, and persuading him to save me the ticket clippings which were swept out of his buses each day. So it seemed a real peace-time wedding—and of course it was quite a help that Addle produced twelve dozen bottles of Veuve Cliquot which he had put by for an emergency.

As the service was beginning who should suddenly appear but Mipsie, who had somehow or other procured bail in order to be at her niece's wedding? It was just like her, but—well, anyway, it wasn't long before the Bishop pronounced the happy pair man and wife, and then with what relief I was able to turn to my beloved sister and give her a loving smile of welcome.

At the reception I introduced Mipsie to her new nephew, to whom I could see she took a great fancy. I heard her say that she had always longed to see the West Indies and how interested she was in coffee plantations. But Paul did not reply. He was looking at Margaret.

And so I come to the end of these letters, happy in the knowledge that my dear daughter is safely married, my dear sister Mipsie may soon be with us again—for an eminent K.C. is defending her and taking the greatest interest in her case, visiting her almost daily, she tells me—and above all that my dear, dear Readers have been able to share, through these pages, in what I like to think of as a fricassee of Noble Life.

Your sincere friend,

BLANCHE ADDLE OF EIGG.